The
NYSTROM
WORLD
ATLAS

NYSTROM

HERFF JONES EDUCATION DIVISION

IN THIS ATLAS

The *Nystrom World Atlas* offers rich coverage of the world, each continent, and key regions. Most continents and regions have two general reference maps.

- **Land cover maps** highlight the big patterns of cropland and other vegetation.
- **Political maps** highlight cities, countries, and other political divisions.

The World and the United States each have a third general reference map.

- **Elevation maps** highlight the big patterns of mountains, lowlands, and landforms.

Thematic maps, graphs, photos, and focus sections provide a closer look at each part of the world. Learn more about these features on pages 3–5.

CONTENTS

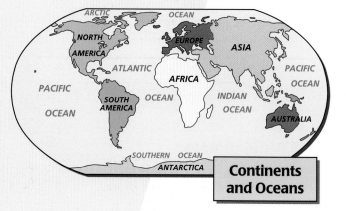

Continents and Oceans

2010 Update of Names and Boundaries
Copyright © 2006, 1999, 1995, 1990 NYSTROM Herff Jones Education Division
4719 W. 62nd St., Indianapolis, Indiana 46268

Printed in U.S.A.
11 10 9 8   13 12 11 10
ISBN-13: 978-0-7825-1076-8   ISBN-10: 0-7825-1076-0
For information about ordering this atlas, 9AW, go to www.nystromnet.com or call 800-621-8086.

Statistics and estimates are from government and United Nations sources: populations for the most recent available date, other data averaged over the three most recent available years.

Land Cover Maps

Colors on the land cover maps show the predominant vegetation on each part of the earth's land surface and the major landforms on land and on the sea floor. Places beyond the map's subject area are in a neutral color.

Detailed Legend for Land Cover Maps

COLOR CATEGORIES

Cropland Grassland Tundra Glacier

Semi-desert & desert | Tropical rain forest | Broadleaf forest | Needleleaf forest

Water and sea floor | Polar sea ice or ice shelf | Land beyond the subject area

MAP FEATURES

N W E S

The compass rose shows the four cardinal directions.

0 250 500 miles
1 inch stands for 730 miles

The scale helps a user estimate distances on a map.

BOUNDARY SYMBOLS

○○○○○○○ Continental boundary
———— International boundary
■■■■■■■ Disputed or undefined boundary
▣ Small country
———— State, province, or territory boundary

LETTERING STYLES

EUROPE — Continent
PACIFIC OCEAN — Ocean
Great Plains — Land feature
Persian Gulf — Water feature
CANADA — Country
TEXAS — State, province, or territory
(U.S.) — National affiliation

CITY SYMBOLS

Chicago ●
Shiraz ●
Cairns ▪

A city's relative size is shown by the size of its symbol and lettering.

Dakar ⊛ — National capital
Atlanta ★ — State, province, or territory capital

OTHER SYMBOLS

Lake and river
Dry or seasonal lake
Waterfall
Canal
Dam
Wetland
Sand dunes
▲ Mountain peak

Political Maps

Colors on the political maps separate one country or state from another. Names of countries, states, and large cities are bold. Many smaller cities also are shown. Non-subject areas have a neutral color.

Detailed Legend for Political Maps

COLOR CATEGORIES

Colors separate different places such as countries or states.

Water | Land beyond the subject area

MAP FEATURES

N W E S

The compass rose shows the four cardinal directions.

0 250 500 miles
1 inch stands for 730 miles

The scale helps a user estimate distances on a map.

BOUNDARY SYMBOLS

○○○○○○○ Continental boundary
———— International boundary
■■■■■■■ Disputed or undefined boundary
▣ Small country
———— State, province, or territory boundary

LETTERING STYLES

UNITED STATES — Country
ALABAMA — State, province, or territory
(U.S.) — National affiliation
ASIA — Continent
ARCTIC OCEAN — Ocean
Sable Island — Land feature
Kara Sea — Water feature

CITY SYMBOLS

Hamburg ●
Rosario ●
Benghazi ▪

A city's relative size is shown by the size of its symbol and lettering.

Dublin ⊛ — National capital
Austin ★ — State, province, or territory capital

OTHER SYMBOLS

Lake and river
Dry or seasonal lake
Waterfall
Canal
Dam

Elevation Maps

Elevation is mapped on reference maps of the World and the United States and on thematic maps of continents. Colors on the elevation maps show land elevations and water depths. Names of major natural features are in bold type.

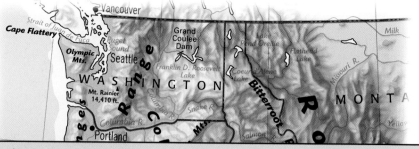

Detailed Legend for Elevation Maps

COLOR CATEGORIES

Feet Above Sea Level

- Over 10,000
- 5,000 to 10,000
- 2,000 to 5,000
- 1,000 to 2,000
- 500 to 1,000
- 0 to 500
- Below sea level

Water Depth in Feet

- Less than 600
- Greater than 600

- Ice covered land
- Land beyond the subject area

BOUNDARY SYMBOLS

- ○○○○○○○○ Continental boundary
- ———— International boundary
- ---------- Disputed or undefined boundary
- ———— State boundary

LETTERING STYLES

AFRICA	Continent
Himalayas	Land feature
INDIAN OCEAN	Ocean
Coral Sea	Water feature
CANADA	Country
TEXAS	State

OTHER SYMBOLS

- Lake and river
- Dry or seasonal lake
- Waterfall
- Canal
- Dam
- Wetland
- ▲ Mountain peak

MAP FEATURES

The compass rose shows the four cardinal directions.

```
0    250    500 miles
1 inch stands for 730 miles
```

The scale helps a user estimate distances on a map.

Thematic Maps

Certain themes are mapped for each continent. Others are mapped just once. The maps that repeat are described in focus sections on pages 14–25. Examples appear below.

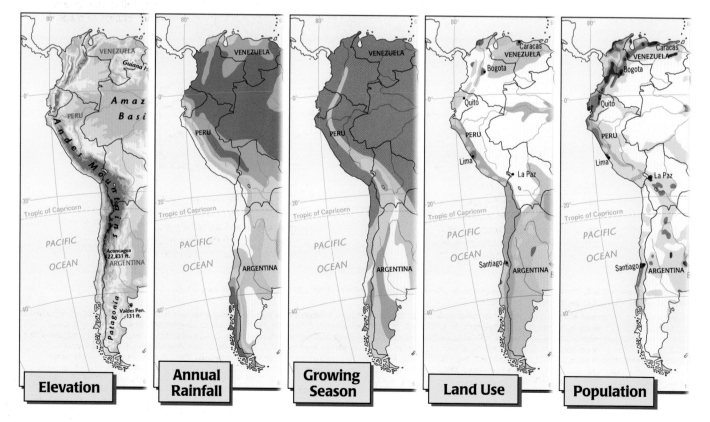

Elevation	Annual Rainfall	Growing Season	Land Use	Population

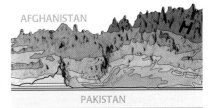

AFGHANISTAN

PAKISTAN

Map Keys

Many of the maps include a key that explains their colors. The same colors can stand for elevations on one map, growing seasons on another, and oil fields on a third. Always read the key before using the map.

Locator Maps

A locator map appears on each two-page spread containing reference maps. Each locator is a small map of the world that shows the position of the continent or region featured on the reference map.

Cross Sections

Special maps and diagrams show a slice of the earth to make continental landscapes and special transportation routes easier to comprehend. Cross sections exaggerate height and depth to make features easy to see.

Size Comparisons

Pairs of maps compare various regions with the familiar size and shape of the contiguous United States. Each pair is drawn to the same scale and is shown as an overlay for ease of comparison.

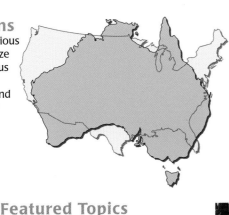

Graphs

The atlas includes circle graphs, bar graphs, and picture graphs. Graphs summarize complex facts in a visual way, making it easier to compare and contrast countries of the world.

Focus on

Featured Topics

Focus sections give special attention to important topics. Those on pages 12–25 introduce themes that are repeated throughout the atlas. On many pages, a bright splash of color marks questions and answers about interesting facts.

Photographs and Diagrams

The book's photographs illustrate the characteristics of people and places around the world. The book's special diagrams illustrate things that cannot be shown in photos or maps.

Map Projections

Map projections are the means by which the curved surface of the earth is transferred to the flat surface of a map. Some of the infinite number of possible projections are explained on pages 106 and 107.

Glossary

The glossary on pages 108 and 109 defines many of the terms used on the maps and graphs and in the text of the atlas. Some of the definitions include page references to photos and special maps in the book.

Sea ice Ice floating on the sea. So permanent cover, mainly near is seasonal. (104)

Sea level The average elevation high and low tide. (14)

Semi-desert Region covered by

ARCTIC OCEAN

Polar Sea Ice

Chukchi
Sea

Bering
Strait

Alaska
(U.S.)

Yukon R.

Mt. McKinley
20,320 ft.

Gulf of Alaska

Kodiak I.

Queen
Charlotte Is.

Vancouver I.

Aleutian Is.

Bering
Sea

60°N

Beaufort
Sea

Banks I.

Mackenzie R.

Victoria I.

ARCTIC CIRCLE 66½°N

Boreal Forest

Rocky Mountains

Great Plains

NORTH

AMERICA

Colorado R.

Rio Grande

Mississippi River

Missouri R.

Great
Lakes

St. Lawrence River

Canadian Shield

Hudson
Bay

Queen Elizabeth Is.

Ellesmere I.

Baffin I.

Baffin
Bay

Hudson Str.

Davis Strait

Greenland

Denmark Strait

Iceland

Cape Farewell

British
Isles

30°N

TROPIC OF CANCER 23½°N

Cape San Lucas

Appalachian Mts.

Gulf of
Mexico

Bahama
Is.

Cuba

West Indies

Central
America

Caribbean Sea

Panama
Canal

ATLANTIC

Azores

Str. of Gibraltar

Canary
Is.

Atlas

S

S

S

Hawaiian
Islands

PACIFIC

N

W   E

S

EQUATOR

Galapagos
Is.

Guiana
Highlands

Amazon

Amazon River

Basin

SOUTH

AMERICA

Andes Mts.

Brazilian
Highlands

EQUATOR

OCEAN

Ascension I.

0°

OCEAN

Tuamotu
Archipelago

TROPIC OF CAPRICORN 23½°S

Pitcairn I.

Easter I.

San Felix I.

San
Ambrosio I.

Aconcagua
22,831 ft.

Pampas

Patagonia

30°S

Juan
Fernandez
Is.

PRIME MERIDIAN

60°S

Falkland Is.

Tierra del Fuego

Cape Horn

South
Georgia I.

SOUTHERN   OCEAN

South
Shetland
Is.

Antarctic
Peninsula

Weddell
Sea

ANTARCTIC

Ross Ice
Shelf

Ronne Ice
Shelf

180°   150°W   120°W   90°W   60°W   30°W   0°

How many oceans are there?

In a sense there is only one World Ocean because it consists of a single interconnected body of water. But scientists say that it has five distinct parts—the five oceans that are named on the map.

Political Map
World

Boundary Symbols

○○○○○○○ Continental boundary

▬▬▬▬▬ International boundary

- - - - - - - Other boundary
(disputed or undefined)

▣ Small country

City Symbols

Shanghai ● ⎫
Vancouver ● ⎬ A city's relative size is
Darwin ● ⎭ shown by the size of
its symbol and lettering.

Cairo ⊛ National capital

Scale at Equator

0   1000   2000 miles

1 inch stands for 1595 miles

Detailed legend on page 3

Who owns Antarctica?

No one does, although seven nations claim parts of it. The United States and many other countries reject these claims. Since Antarctica is not owned by any country, it is not shown in any of the map's political colors.

Elevation Map
World

Feet Above Sea Level

- Over 10,000
- 5,000 to 10,000
- 2,000 to 5,000
- 1,000 to 2,000
- 500 to 1,000
- 0 to 500
- Below sea level

Water Depth in Feet

- Less than 600
- Greater than 600

Boundary Symbols

- ○○○○○○○○ Continental boundary
- ——— International boundary
- ------- Other boundary (disputed or undefined)

Scale at Equator

0   1000   2000 miles

1 inch stands for 1595 miles

Detailed legend on page 4

Can rivers flow up?

If *up* means "up the map" or "north," the answer is yes. Rivers can flow in any compass direction, as long as it is downhill. You can use an elevation map's colors to tell which direction a river flows.

Focus on Land Cover

- Land cover maps show the most widespread material on the earth's surface.
- Most land is covered with plants. This includes crops planted by people as well as natural vegetation.
- Icy glaciers cover areas that are very cold. Deserts with little or no vegetation cover areas that are very dry.

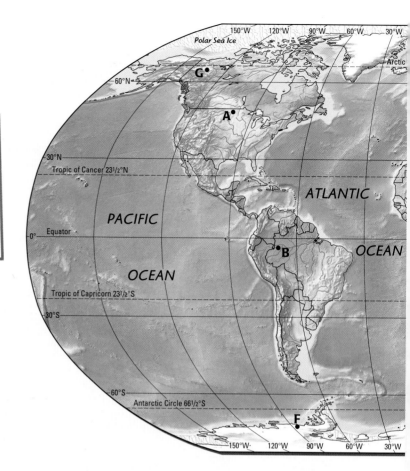

A **Cropland** Large areas that are mainly covered with crops may also include roads, small livestock farms, woodlots, and human settlements of any size.

B **Tropical rain forest** Hot, wet regions near the Equator have broadleaf forests that are green all year. These forests are thick with large trees and other plants.

C **Grassland** Vast areas mainly covered with grass are often used as grazing land. Some grasslands also have scattered trees or shrubs.

D **Semi-desert and desert** Dry areas may be covered with shrubs or cactus. The driest areas have little or no vegetation of any kind.

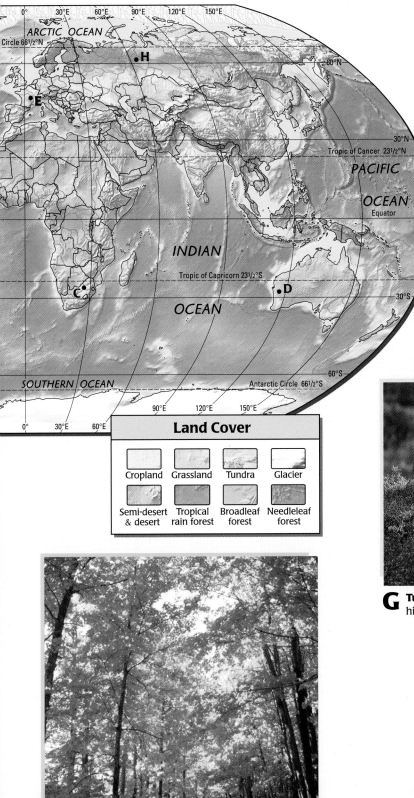

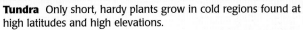

Land Cover

Cropland	Grassland	Tundra	Glacier
Semi-desert & desert	Tropical rain forest	Broadleaf forest	Needleleaf forest

F **Glacier** Continental and mountain glaciers form near the North and South Poles and on high mountains. They cover land with ice for hundreds or thousands of years.

G **Tundra** Only short, hardy plants grow in cold regions found at high latitudes and high elevations.

E **Broadleaf forest** Broadleaf trees in cool and cold climates lose their leaves each fall. On the map, this category also includes forests that are a mixture of broadleaf and needleleaf trees.

H **Needleleaf forest** Most needleleaf trees are evergreen, such as pine, spruce, and fir trees. But some are deciduous.

Focus on Elevation and Landforms

- *Elevation* is distance above sea level. Water flows from higher elevations down to the sea.

- *Landforms* are natural features of the land. Most landforms are shaped by flowing water.

- Many landforms have distinctive shapes and elevation patterns that can be seen on cross sections and elevation maps.

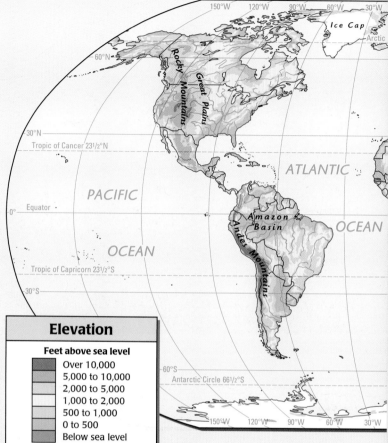

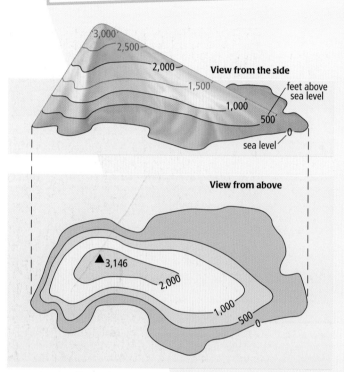

Colors on elevation maps stand for different distances above sea level. These two views show the same island. The view from above is able to show both the island's height and its shape using color alone.

Hills Hills rise to higher elevations than the land around them. Most are rounded and not steep. Hilly land may seem lumpy.

Tablelands Tablelands—also called *plateaus*—are fairly level except where rivers have carved canyons. Tablelands have high elevations, although nearby mountains may be higher.

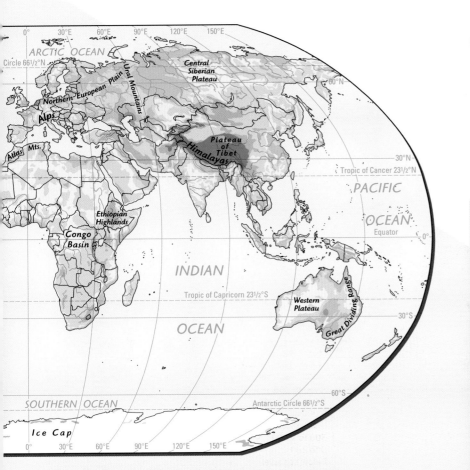

How Tall Is Tall?

Mount Everest is the world's highest mountain at 29,035 feet above sea level. But Hawaii's Mauna Kea volcano is tallest, rising at least 32,000 feet from the deep sea floor to its summit at 13,796 feet above sea level.

Widely spaced mountains Sometimes single mountains stand alone or far apart from one another, surrounded by lower land. Like this one, many of these mountains are volcanoes.

Plains and basins *Plains* are vast areas that are gently rolling or nearly level, often at low elevations. *Basins* are level lands surrounded by mountains.

Mountain ranges Mountains in long lines or large groups are called *mountain ranges*. Their summits are much higher than the lands below.

Focus on Rainfall

- All living things need water. Where rain is scarce, life is limited.
- Rainfall varies greatly from one part of the world to another.
- The pattern of rainfall affects not only what grows but also how and where people live.

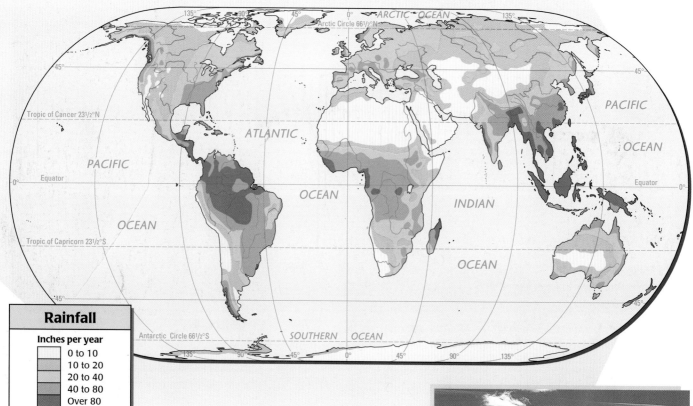

Rainfall

Inches per year
	0 to 10
	10 to 20
	20 to 40
	40 to 80
	Over 80

Annual rainfall is the average total precipitation for a year.

Geographers count the water from melted snow, hail, and sleet as rainfall.

Focus on Temperature

- The longest stretch of days with air temperatures above freezing is a region's *growing season*.
- The growing season is the time of year when crops can grow.
- Some places are hot or cold all year. Others have seasons.

How Cold Was It?

The coldest temperature on record is -128.6°F. It was measured at Vostok, a Russian research station in Antarctica.

In the tropics, winter may be as hot as summer.

Away from the tropics, winter is cold. In many places it is snowy too.

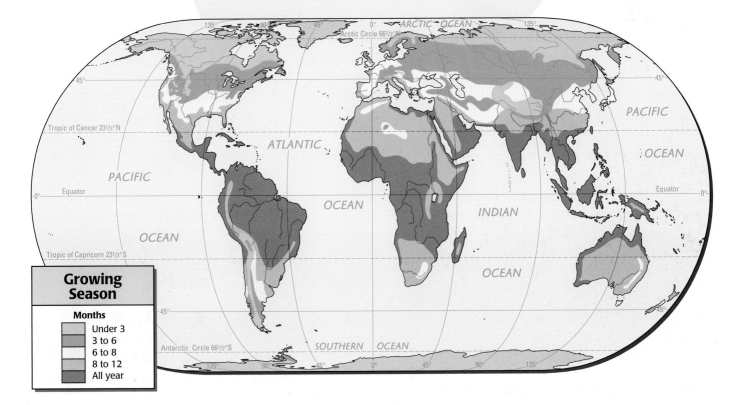

Growing Season

Months

- Under 3
- 3 to 6
- 6 to 8
- 8 to 12
- All year

Focus on Climate

- Climate strongly affects where and how people live.
- Rainfall and temperature are the most important elements of climate.
- Latitude, distance from the ocean, and elevation affect a region's climate by affecting rainfall, temperature, and wind.

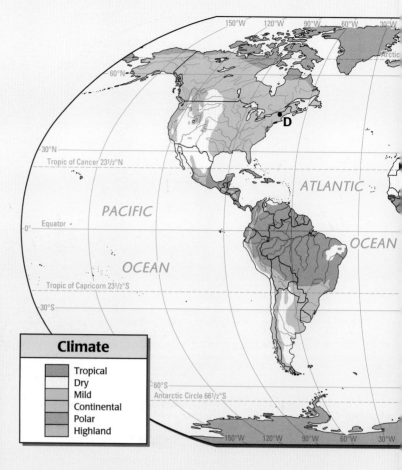

Climate

- Tropical
- Dry
- Mild
- Continental
- Polar
- Highland

A **Tropical climates** Regions in this category are hot all year. Some tropical regions also are rainy all year, while others have dry seasons.

B **Dry climates** Semi-deserts or *steppes* are dry but get occasional rain. True deserts are very dry all year. Dry regions may be warm to hot all year, or may vary with the seasons.

C **Mild climates** Regions with mild climates have rainy winters that are mild to cool. Summers vary from warm to hot and may be dry or wet.

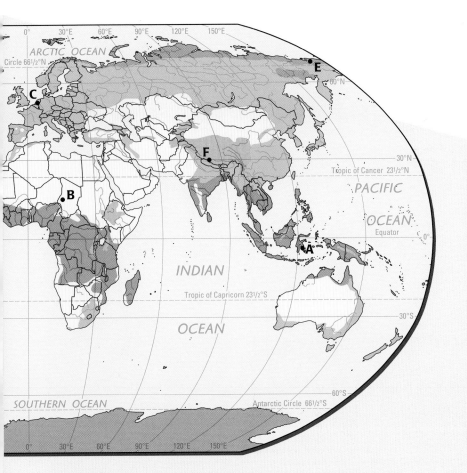

F **Highland climates** Local climates vary greatly because of differences in elevation. Distance from the Equator also affects highland climates.

D **Continental climates** Places in this category have wet summers that are cool in some regions and hot in others. Winters are cold to very cold and snowy to very snowy.

E **Polar climates** Tundra and ice cap regions have polar climates. They get little snow and even less rain and are cool to very cold all year.

Focus on Land Use

- Providing food is the main way that most land is used.
- Commercial farming, ranching, and most herding produce food that is sold for profit.
- Subsistence farmers and nomadic herders produce food mainly for their own families to eat.
- Urban land use includes trade, manufacturing, financial services, and other activities of cities and suburbs.

A **Commercial farming** Modern orchards, vast fields of crops, and dairy farms rely on machinery.

B **Subsistence farming** Most subsistence farmers have small pieces of land. Few have modern machinery.

C **Ranching or herding** Ranchers, who are called *herders* in some countries, raise herds of grazing animals.

D **Nomadic herding** In an annual cycle, nomads move with their herds from one seasonal source of food and water to another.

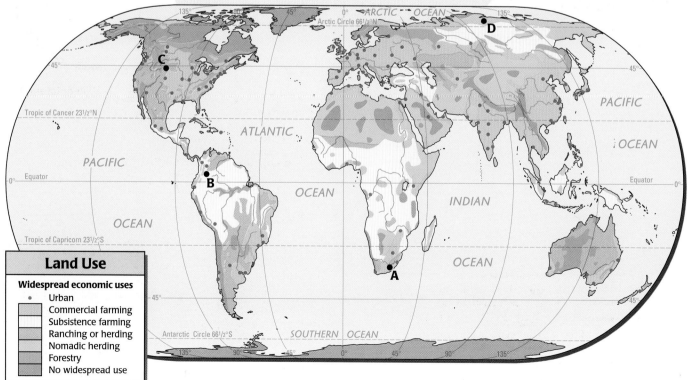

Land Use

Widespread economic uses

- Urban
- Commercial farming
- Subsistence farming
- Ranching or herding
- Nomadic herding
- Forestry
- No widespread use

Focus on Food Resources

- Cereal grains, all in the grass family, feed more people than any other kind of food.
- Rice grows only with lots of water. Millet needs little water.
- Wheat is used for an amazing variety of breads and noodles.
- Corn, also known as *maize*, feeds both people and livestock.

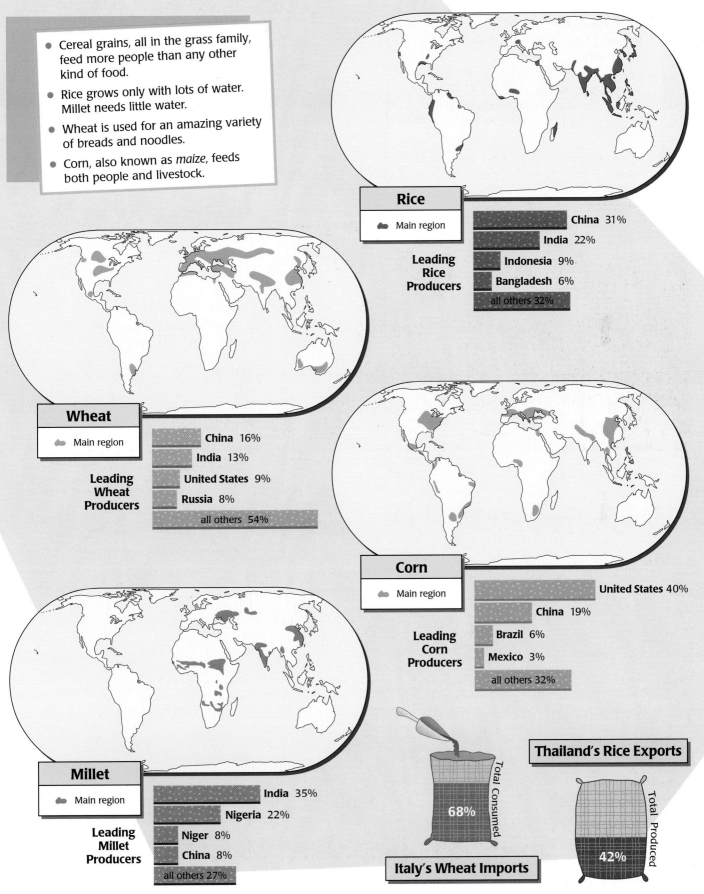

Rice

🐖 Main region

Leading Rice Producers

China 31%
India 22%
Indonesia 9%
Bangladesh 6%
all others 32%

Wheat

🐖 Main region

Leading Wheat Producers

China 16%
India 13%
United States 9%
Russia 8%
all others 54%

Corn

🐖 Main region

Leading Corn Producers

United States 40%
China 19%
Brazil 6%
Mexico 3%
all others 32%

Millet

🐖 Main region

Leading Millet Producers

India 35%
Nigeria 22%
Niger 8%
China 8%
all others 27%

Italy's Wheat Imports

Total Consumed
68%

Thailand's Rice Exports

Total Produced
42%

Focus on Energy Resources

- Coal, oil, natural gas, and uranium fill most of the world's energy needs.
- All four are *consumable*. Once used, they are gone forever.
- Of the four, coal is the most widespread and cheapest to use.
- Since coal, oil, and natural gas all were once ancient plants, they are known as *fossil fuels*.

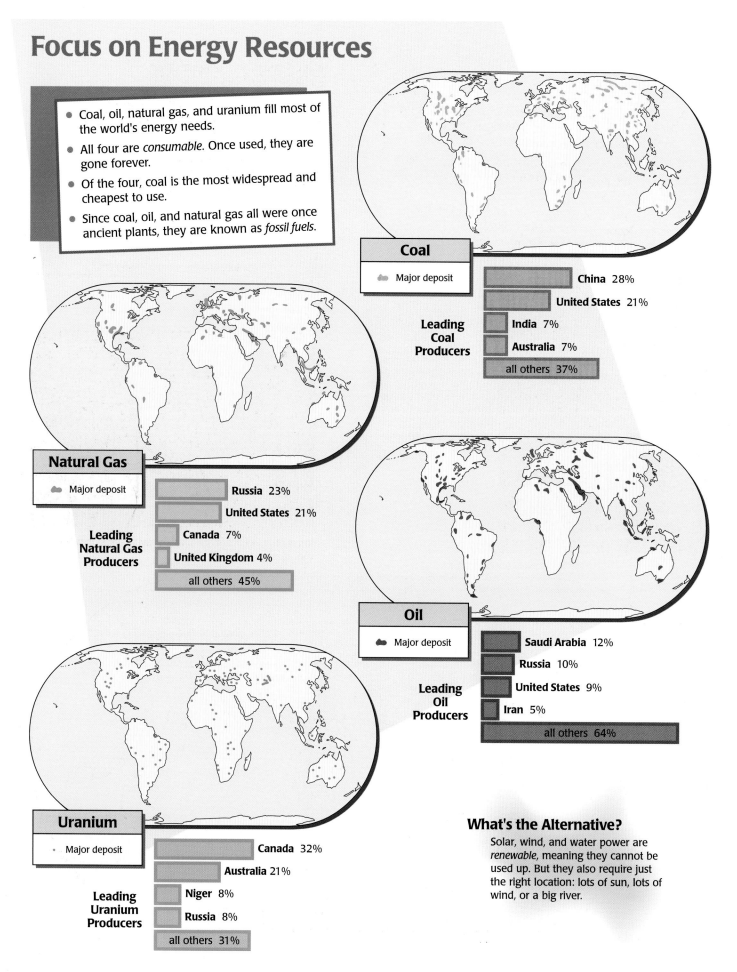

Coal

🔷 Major deposit

Leading Coal Producers

China	28%
United States	21%
India	7%
Australia	7%
all others	37%

Natural Gas

☁ Major deposit

Leading Natural Gas Producers

Russia	23%
United States	21%
Canada	7%
United Kingdom	4%
all others	45%

Oil

🔷 Major deposit

Leading Oil Producers

Saudi Arabia	12%
Russia	10%
United States	9%
Iran	5%
all others	64%

Uranium

· Major deposit

Leading Uranium Producers

Canada	32%
Australia	21%
Niger	8%
Russia	8%
all others	31%

What's the Alternative?

Solar, wind, and water power are *renewable*, meaning they cannot be used up. But they also require just the right location: lots of sun, lots of wind, or a big river.

Focus on Standard of Living

- A country's *standard of living* depends on the level of goods and services available to meet the needs and wants of its people.

- One measure of standard of living compares the number of cars and the number of people.

- The fewer people per car, the higher the country's standard of living.

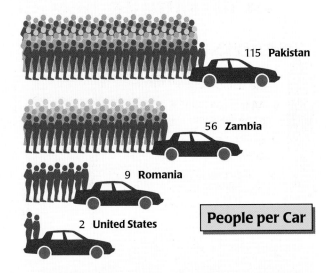

115 **Pakistan**

56 **Zambia**

9 **Romania**

2 **United States**

People per Car

In prosperous countries, an average family can afford a car. Many families own more than one car.

In countries with low standards of living, most families cannot afford a car at all.

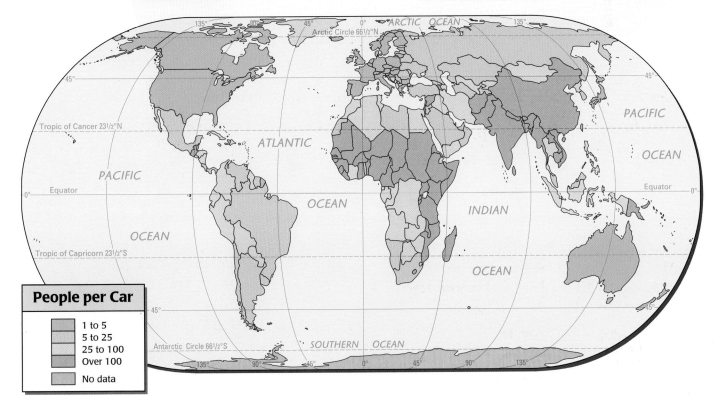

People per Car

- 1 to 5
- 5 to 25
- 25 to 100
- Over 100
- No data

Focus on Population

- The world has about 6.5 billion people—and 8,400 more are born every hour.
- Despite these numbers, only certain regions of the world are densely populated.
- Areas that are very cold or very dry are sparsely populated and likely to remain so.

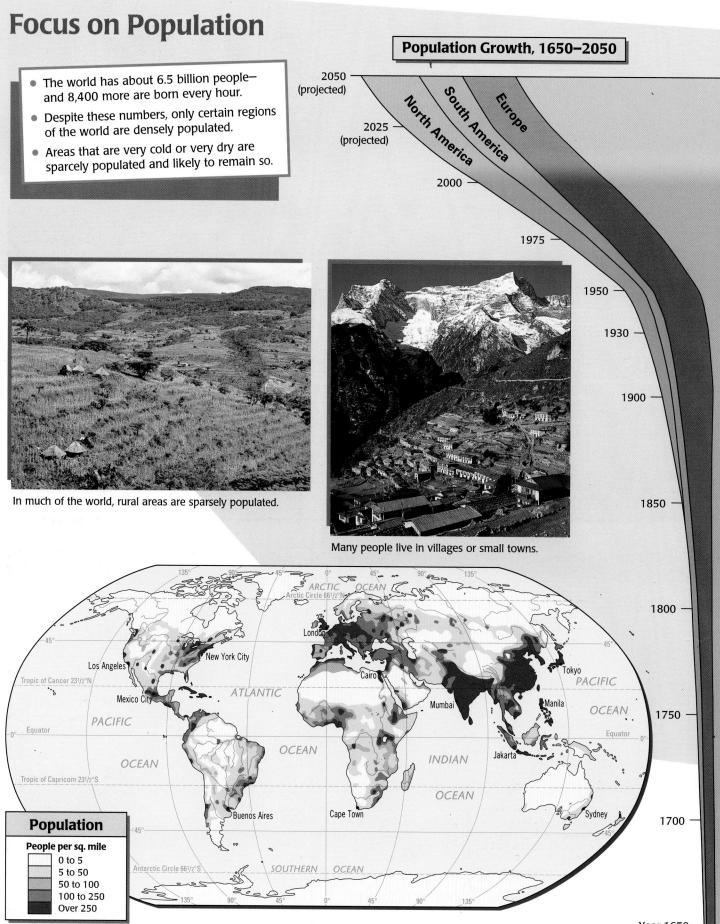

In much of the world, rural areas are sparsely populated.

Many people live in villages or small towns.

Population Growth, 1650–2050

North America
South America
Europe

2050 (projected)
2025 (projected)
2000
1975
1950
1930
1900
1850
1800
1750
1700
Year 1650

Population

People per sq. mile

- 0 to 5
- 5 to 50
- 50 to 100
- 100 to 250
- Over 250

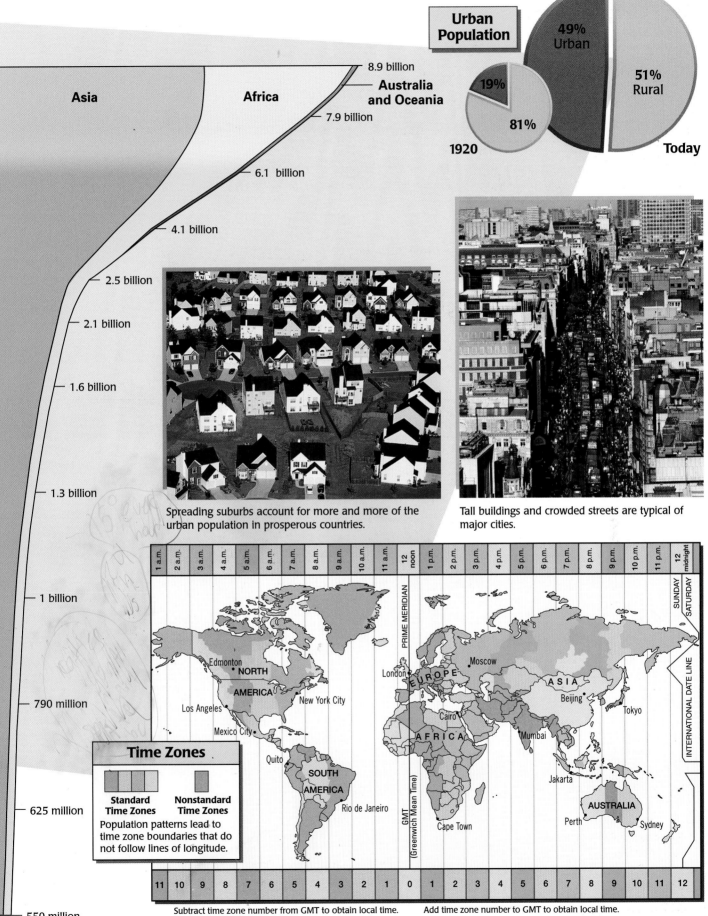

Asia

Africa

8.9 billion

Australia and Oceania

7.9 billion

6.1 billion

4.1 billion

2.5 billion

2.1 billion

1.6 billion

1.3 billion

1 billion

790 million

625 million

550 million

Urban Population

49% Urban

51% Rural

19%

81%

1920

Today

Spreading suburbs account for more and more of the urban population in prosperous countries.

Tall buildings and crowded streets are typical of major cities.

| 1 a.m. | 2 a.m. | 3 a.m. | 4 a.m. | 5 a.m. | 6 a.m. | 7 a.m. | 8 a.m. | 9 a.m. | 10 a.m. | 11 a.m. | 12 noon | 1 p.m. | 2 p.m. | 3 p.m. | 4 p.m. | 5 p.m. | 6 p.m. | 7 p.m. | 8 p.m. | 9 p.m. | 10 p.m. | 11 p.m. | 12 midnight |

PRIME MERIDIAN

SUNDAY
SATURDAY

Edmonton
• NORTH
AMERICA

Los Angeles

New York City

London EUROPE

Moscow

ASIA

Beijing

Tokyo

Mexico City •

Cairo

Mumbai

AFRICA

Jakarta

INTERNATIONAL DATE LINE

Time Zones

Quito

SOUTH
AMERICA

Rio de Janeiro

Cape Town

GMT (Greenwich Mean Time)

AUSTRALIA

Perth

Sydney

Standard Time Zones **Nonstandard Time Zones**

Population patterns lead to time zone boundaries that do not follow lines of longitude.

| 11 | 10 | 9 | 8 | 7 | 6 | 5 | 4 | 3 | 2 | 1 | 0 | 1 | 2 | 3 | 4 | 5 | 6 | 7 | 8 | 9 | 10 | 11 | 12 |

Subtract time zone number from GMT to obtain local time.   Add time zone number to GMT to obtain local time.

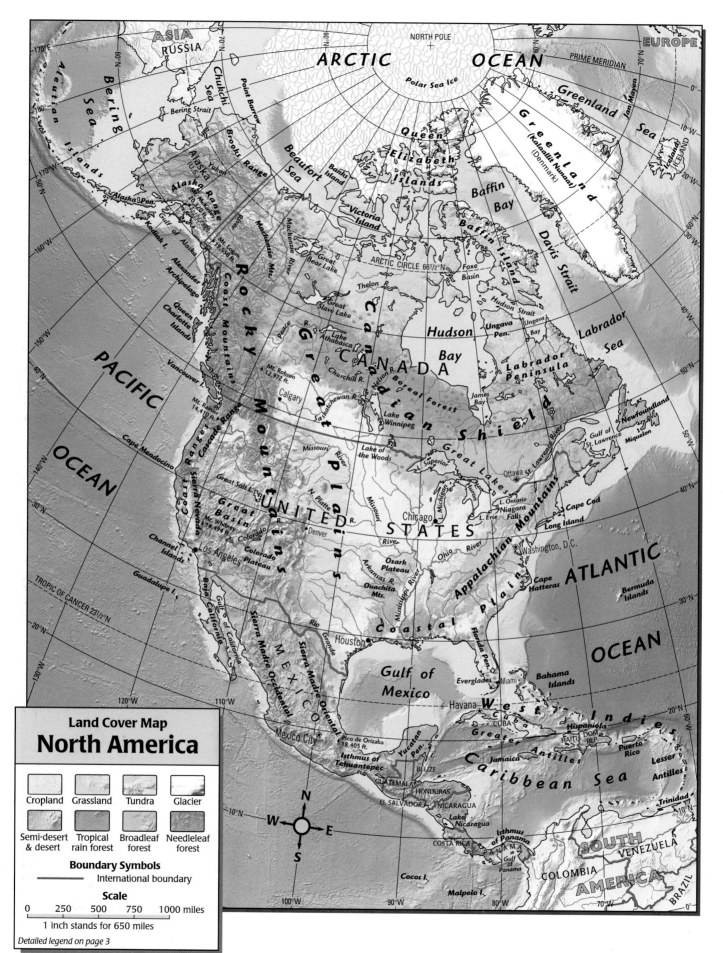

Land Cover Map
North America

Cropland **Grassland** **Tundra** **Glacier**

Semi-desert & desert **Tropical rain forest** **Broadleaf forest** **Needleleaf forest**

Boundary Symbols
International boundary

Scale
0 250 500 750 1000 miles
1 inch stands for 650 miles

Detailed legend on page 3

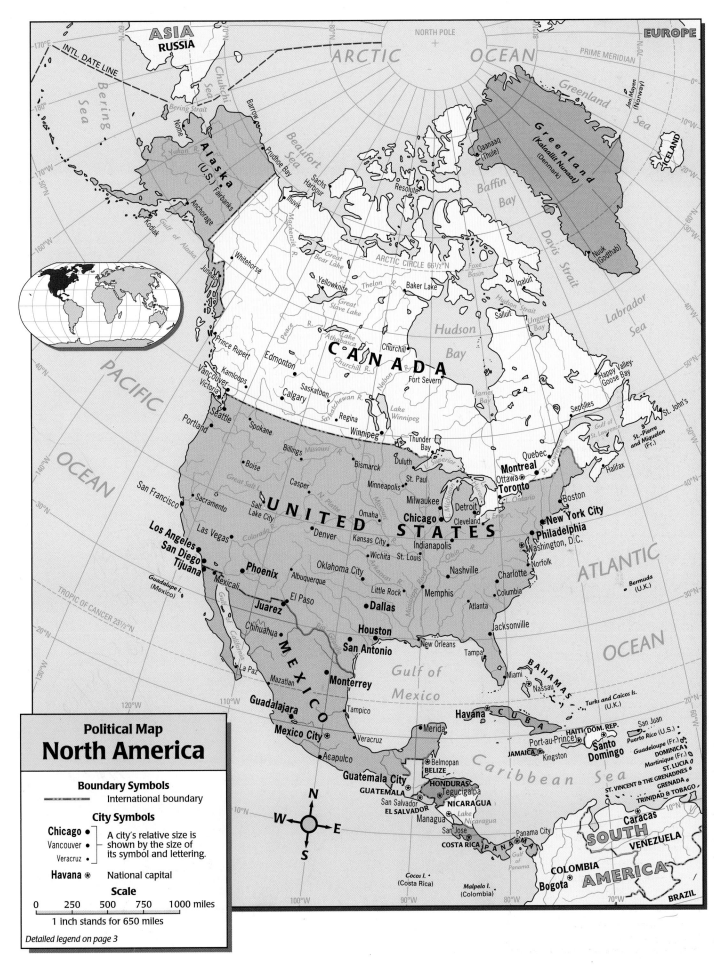

Political Map
North America

Boundary Symbols
— · — · — · International boundary

City Symbols

Chicago ● ┐
Vancouver ● ┤ A city's relative size is shown by the size of its symbol and lettering.
Veracruz ● ┘

Havana ⊛ National capital

Scale

0   250   500   750   1000 miles

1 inch stands for 650 miles

Detailed legend on page 3

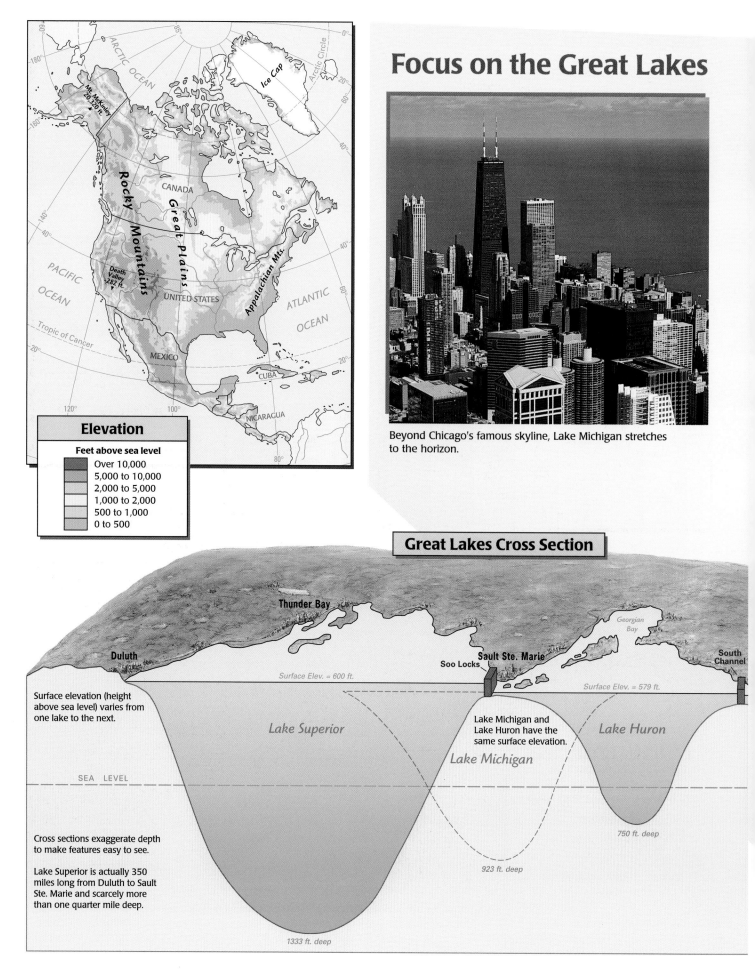

Elevation

Feet above sea level

- Over 10,000
- 5,000 to 10,000
- 2,000 to 5,000
- 1,000 to 2,000
- 500 to 1,000
- 0 to 500

Focus on the Great Lakes

Beyond Chicago's famous skyline, Lake Michigan stretches to the horizon.

Great Lakes Cross Section

Surface elevation (height above sea level) varies from one lake to the next.

Lake Michigan and Lake Huron have the same surface elevation.

Cross sections exaggerate depth to make features easy to see.

Lake Superior is actually 350 miles long from Duluth to Sault Ste. Marie and scarcely more than one quarter mile deep.

Thunder Bay
Duluth
Georgian Bay
Sault Ste. Marie
Soo Locks
South Channel

Surface Elev. = 600 ft.
Surface Elev. = 579 ft.

SEA LEVEL

Lake Superior
Lake Michigan
Lake Huron

1333 ft. deep
923 ft. deep
750 ft. deep

- The five Great Lakes are large enough to be called *inland seas*.
- They connect to form North America's most important inland waterway. The St. Lawrence River links them with the Atlantic Ocean.
- For centuries the Great Lakes have been used for transporting raw materials and finished goods.

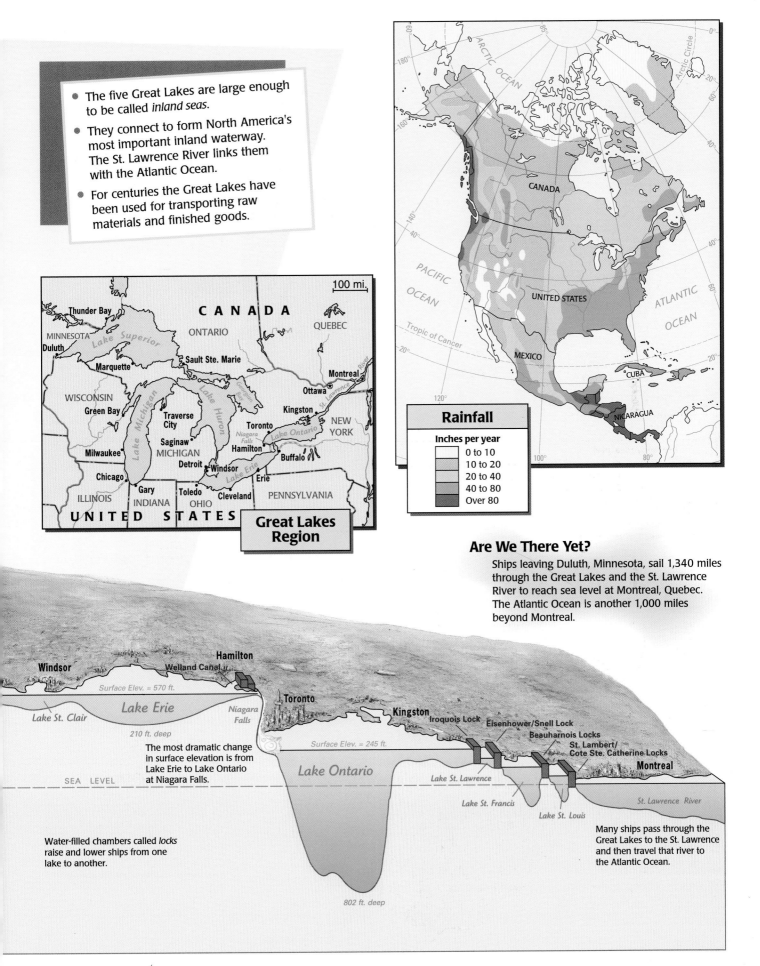

Great Lakes Region

100 mi.

Rainfall

Inches per year

- 0 to 10
- 10 to 20
- 20 to 40
- 40 to 80
- Over 80

Are We There Yet?

Ships leaving Duluth, Minnesota, sail 1,340 miles through the Great Lakes and the St. Lawrence River to reach sea level at Montreal, Quebec. The Atlantic Ocean is another 1,000 miles beyond Montreal.

Windsor

Hamilton

Welland Canal

Surface Elev. = 570 ft.

Lake St. Clair

Lake Erie

Niagara Falls

Lake St. Clair

Lake Erie

210 ft. deep

The most dramatic change in surface elevation is from Lake Erie to Lake Ontario at Niagara Falls.

Toronto

Kingston

Iroquois Lock

Eisenhower/Snell Lock

Beauharnois Locks

St. Lambert/ Cote Ste. Catherine Locks

Montreal

Surface Elev. = 245 ft.

Lake Ontario

Lake St. Lawrence

SEA LEVEL

Lake St. Francis

Lake St. Louis

St. Lawrence River

Water-filled chambers called *locks* raise and lower ships from one lake to another.

Many ships pass through the Great Lakes to the St. Lawrence and then travel that river to the Atlantic Ocean.

802 ft. deep

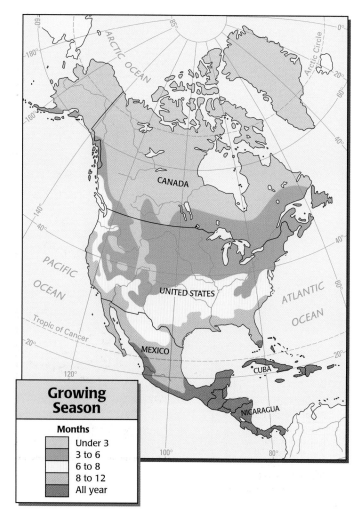

Growing Season

Months
- Under 3
- 3 to 6
- 6 to 8
- 8 to 12
- All year

What's Green About That?

Most of Greenland is icy white, not green. The glacier that covers most of the island is as vast as the Gulf of Mexico and contains about the same amount of water.

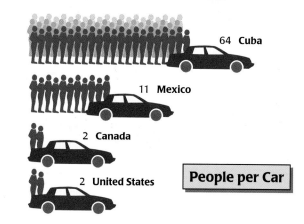

64 **Cuba**

11 **Mexico**

2 **Canada**

2 **United States**

People per Car

Large areas of North America are used as grazing land for herds of cattle.

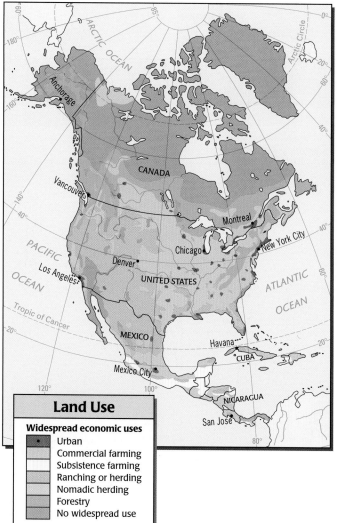

Land Use

Widespread economic uses
- Urban
- Commercial farming
- Subsistence farming
- Ranching or herding
- Nomadic herding
- Forestry
- No widespread use

The ancestors of most North Americans came from Europe. But people here represent every other part of the world too.

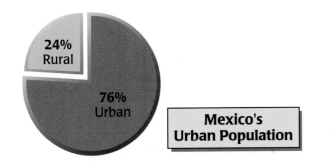

24% Rural

76% Urban

Mexico's Urban Population

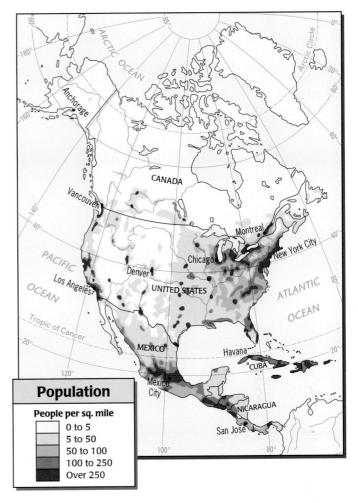

Population

People per sq. mile

0 to 5
5 to 50
50 to 100
100 to 250
Over 250

Focus on Neighboring Countries

Canada's Size and Shape

- Canada, the United States, and Mexico are by far the largest countries in North America.
- These neighbors share borders that are thousands of miles long.
- Both Canada and Mexico are major trading partners with the United States.

Mexico's Size and Shape

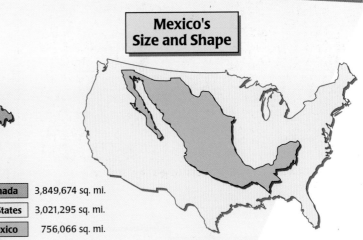

Canada	3,849,674 sq. mi.
48 States	3,021,295 sq. mi.
Mexico	756,066 sq. mi.

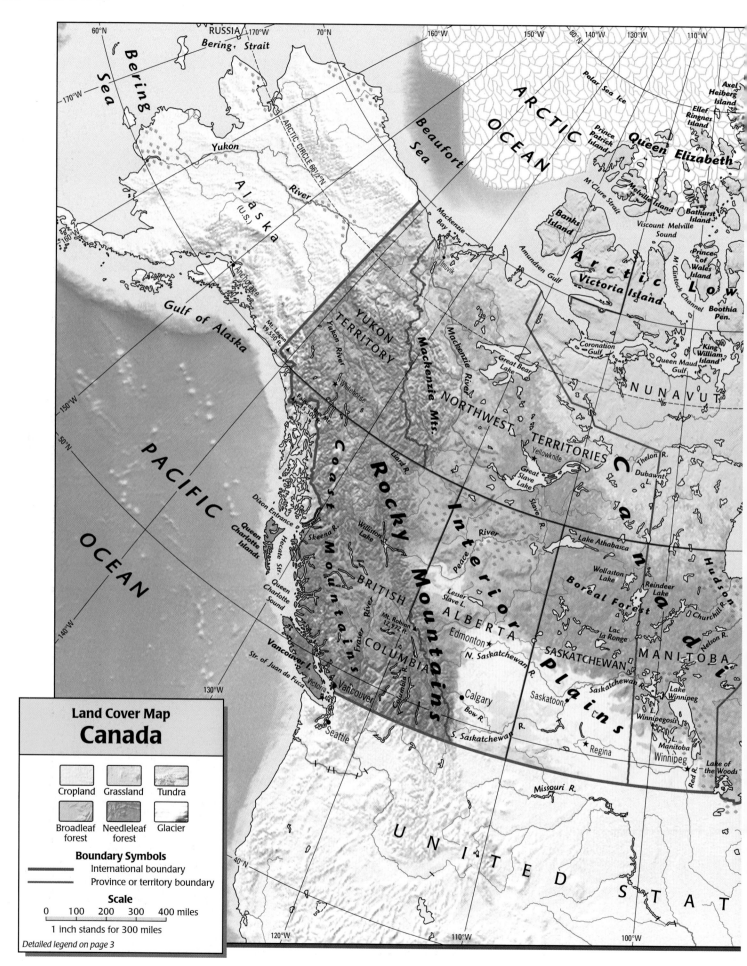

RUSSIA
Bering Strait
Bering Sea
Yukon
ARCTIC CIRCLE 66½°N
Yukon River
Alaska (U.S.)
Anchorage
Gulf of Alaska
Beaufort Sea
Mackenzie Bay
Inuvik
ARCTIC OCEAN
Polar Sea Ice
Prince Patrick Island
Banks Island
M'Clure Strait
Melville Island
Viscount Melville Sound
Amundsen Gulf
Victoria Island
Coronation Gulf
Queen Maud Gulf
Axel Heiberg Island
Ellef Ringnes Island
Queen Elizabeth
Bathurst Island
Prince of Wales Island
M'Clintock Channel
King William Island
Boothia Pen.
Arctic Low

Mt. Logan 19,550 ft.
YUKON TERRITORY
Yukon River
Whitehorse
Fairweather Mt. 15,300 ft.
Mackenzie Mts.
Mackenzie River
Liard R.
NORTHWEST TERRITORIES
Great Bear Lake
Yellowknife
Great Slave Lake
NUNAVUT
Thelon R.
Dubawnt L.
Slave R.
Canada

PACIFIC OCEAN

Dixon Entrance
Queen Charlotte Islands
Hecate Str.
Skeena R.
Coast Mountains
Queen Charlotte Sound
Williston Lake
Rocky Mountains
Fraser River
Mt. Robson 12,972 ft.
BRITISH COLUMBIA
Interior Plains
Peace River
Lesser Slave L.
ALBERTA
Edmonton
N. Saskatchewan R.
Calgary
Bow R.
S. Saskatchewan R.
River
Lake Athabasca
Wollaston Lake
Lac la Ronge
SASKATCHEWAN
Boreal Forest
Reindeer Lake
Churchill R.
Saskatoon
Saskatchewan R.
Regina
Hudson
Nelson R.
MANITOBA
L. Winnipegosis
Lake Winnipeg
Manitoba
Winnipeg
Red R.
Lake of the Woods

Vancouver I.
Str. of Juan de Fuca
Victoria
Vancouver
Columbia R.
Seattle
Missouri R.
UNITED STATES

Land Cover Map
Canada

Cropland Grassland Tundra

Broadleaf forest Needleleaf forest Glacier

Boundary Symbols
International boundary
Province or territory boundary

Scale
0   100   200   300   400 miles
1 inch stands for 300 miles

Detailed legend on page 3

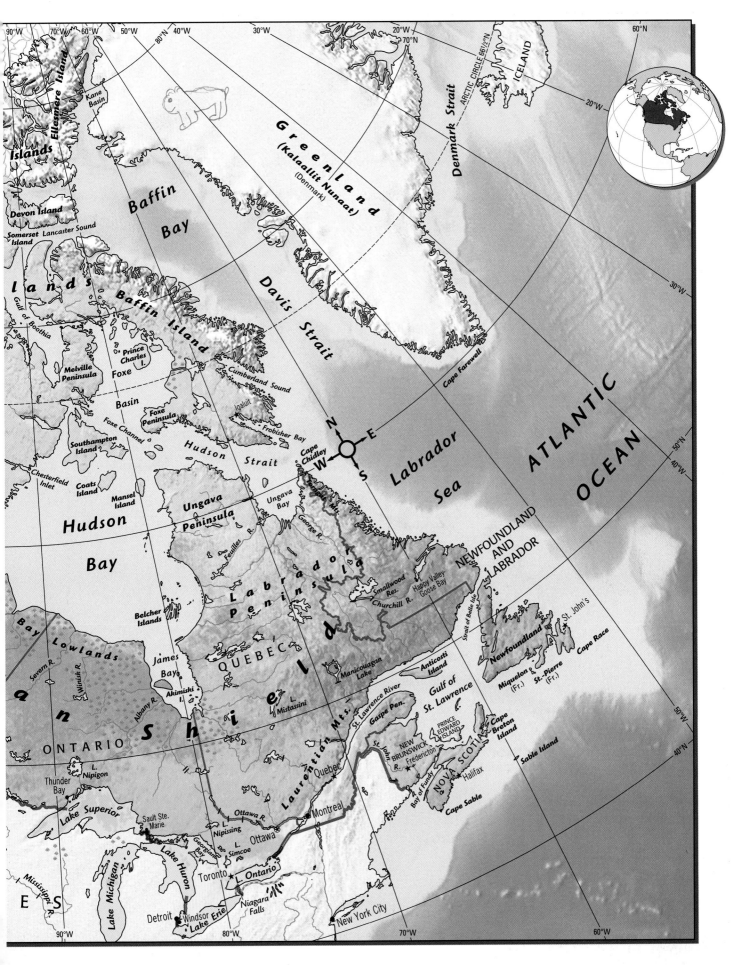

90°W 70°W 60°W 50°W 40°W 30°W 20°W 60°N
80°N 70°N

Ellesmere Island

Islands

Kane Basin

Devon Island

Somerset Island Lancaster Sound

G r e e n l a n d
(Kalaallit Nunaat)
(Denmark)

ICELAND

ARCTIC CIRCLE 66½°N

20°W

Denmark Strait

Baffin Bay

l a n d s

Gulf of Boothia

Baffin Island

Davis Strait

30°W

Melville Peninsula

Prince Charles I.

Foxe

Cumberland Sound

Cape Farewell

Basin

Foxe Peninsula

Iqaluit

Foxe Channel

Frobisher Bay

Southampton Island

Hudson Strait

N

E

Labrador Sea

ATLANTIC

50°N

OCEAN

40°W

Chesterfield Inlet

Coats Island

Mansel Island

Cape Chidley

W

S

Torngat Mts.

Hudson

Ungava Peninsula

Ungava Bay

George R.

NEWFOUNDLAND AND LABRADOR

Bay

Belcher Islands

Feuilles

L a b r a d o r
P e n i n s u l a

Smallwood Res.

Happy Valley-Goose Bay

Churchill R.

St. John's

Bay Lowlands

James Bay

QUÉBEC

Manicouagan Lake

Anticosti Island

Strait of Belle Isle

Newfoundland

Cape Race

Severn R.

Winisk R.

Albany R.

Akimiski I.

L. Mistassini

St. Lawrence River

Gulf of St. Lawrence

Miquelon (Fr.)

St.-Pierre (Fr.)

a n S h i e l d

ONTARIO

Laurentian Mts.

Gaspé Pen.

PRINCE EDWARD ISLAND

Cape Breton Island

50°N

Sable Island

40°N

Thunder Bay

L. Nipigon

Québec

St. John R.

NEW BRUNSWICK

Fredericton

NOVA SCOTIA

Halifax

Lake Superior

Sault Ste. Marie

Ottawa R.

Montréal

Bay of Fundy

Cape Sable

Nipissing

Georgian Bay

L. Simcoe

L. Ottawa

E S

Mississippi R.

Lake Michigan

Lake Huron

Toronto

L. Ontario

Niagara Falls

New York City

Detroit

Windsor

Lake Erie

90°W 80°W 70°W 60°W

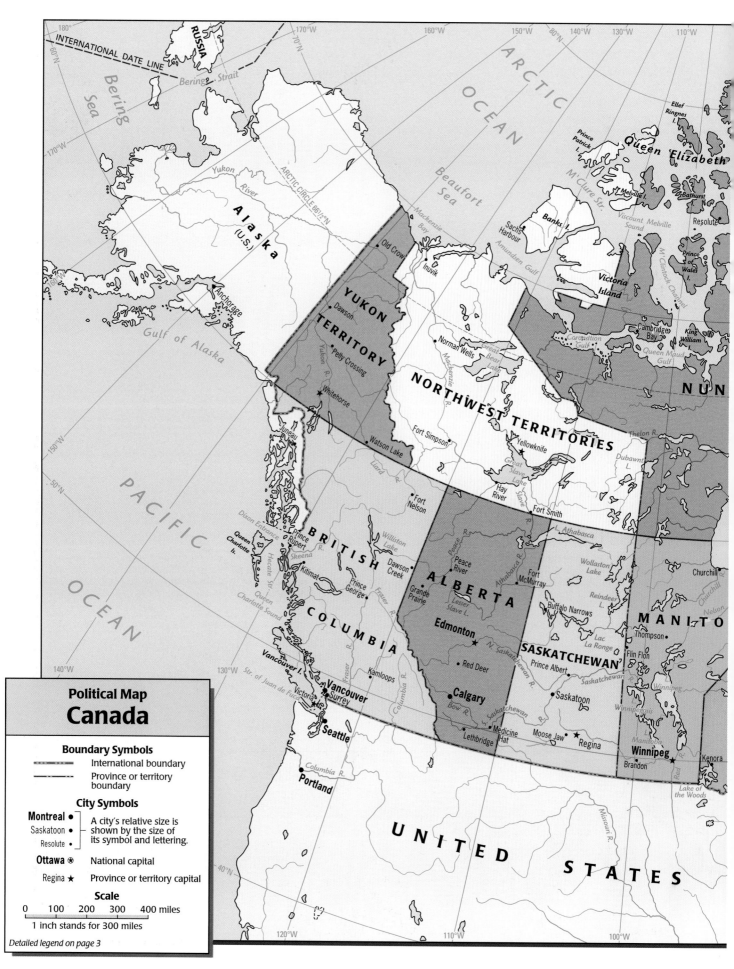

INTERNATIONAL DATE LINE

RUSSIA

Bering Strait

Bering Sea

ARCTIC OCEAN

Beaufort Sea

Prince Patrick I.

Ellef Ringnes I.

Queen Elizabeth

Melville I.

Bathurst

Viscount Melville Sound

Resolute

Yukon River

Banks I.

Sachs Harbour

M'Clure Str.

Prince of Wales I.

ARCTIC CIRCLE 66½°N

Amundsen Gulf

Victoria Island

M'Clintock Channel

Old Crow

Inuvik

Mackenzie Bay

Coronation Gulf

Cambridge Bay

King William I.

Alaska (U.S.)

YUKON TERRITORY

Dawson

Pelly Crossing

Norman Wells

Great Bear Lake

Queen Maud Gulf

NUN

Anchorage

Yukon R.

Mackenzie R.

NORTHWEST TERRITORIES

Gulf of Alaska

Whitehorse

Juneau

Watson Lake

Fort Simpson

Yellowknife

Great Slave Lake

Thelon R.

Dubawnt L.

Liard

Fort Nelson

Hay River

Slave R.

Fort Smith

Athabasca

Wollaston Lake

PACIFIC OCEAN

Dixon Entrance

Queen Charlotte Is.

Prince Rupert

Hecate Str.

Skeena

Kitimat

Williston Lake

Dawson Creek

Prince George

Fraser

BRITISH COLUMBIA

Peace River

Peace R.

Athabasca R.

Fort McMurray

Reindeer L.

Churchill

MANITO

Queen Charlotte Sound

ALBERTA

Grande Prairie

Lesser Slave L.

Buffalo Narrows

Lac La Ronge

Nelson

Vancouver I.

Edmonton

Red Deer

N. Saskatchewan R.

SASKATCHEWAN

Prince Albert

Thompson

Flin Flon

Kamloops

Columbia R.

Calgary

Bow R.

Saskatoon

Saskatchewan R.

Winnipegosis

Victoria

Vancouver

Surrey

Fraser

Lethbridge

Medicine Hat

Moose Jaw

Regina

Winnipeg

Str. of Juan de Fuca

Seattle

Columbia R.

Portland

UNITED STATES

Missouri R.

Brandon

Kenora

Lake of the Woods

Axel Heiberg I.

Ellesmere Island

Islands

Kane Basin

Qaanaaq (Thule)

Devon I.

Lancaster Sound

Somerset

Gulf of Boothia

Kugaaruk

Baffin Bay

Clyde River

Baffin Island

Foxe Basin

Greenland (Kalaallit Nunaat) (Denmark)

Denmark Strait

ICELAND

ARCTIC CIRCLE 66½°N

Davis Strait

Cumberland Sd.

Iqaluit

NAVUT

Southampton I.

Chesterfield Inlet

Coats I.

Foxe Channel

Salluit

Probisher Bay

Rankin Inlet

Mansel I.

Hudson Strait

Ungava Bay

Labrador Sea

ATLANTIC

Hudson Bay

Feuilles R.

Kuujjuaq

George R.

OCEAN

BA

Fort Severn

Belcher Is.

Kuujjuarapik

Smallwood Res.

Happy Valley-Goose Bay

Churchill R.

NEWFOUNDLAND AND LABRADOR

Severn R.

Winisk

James Bay

Albany R.

Moosonee

L. Mistassini

Labrador City

Sept-Îles

Anticosti I.

Manicouagan Lake

Corner Brook

Newfoundland

St. John's

ONTARIO

QUEBEC

St. Lawrence R.

Gulf of St. Lawrence

St.-Pierre and Miquelon (France)

L. Nipigon

Saguenay

Val-d'Or

Quebec

PRINCE EDWARD ISLAND

Charlottetown

Cape Breton I.

Thunder Bay

Ottawa R.

Gatineau

Montreal

NEW BRUNSWICK

Fredericton

NOVA SCOTIA

Sable I. (Nova Scotia)

Lake Superior

Sault Ste. Marie

Sudbury

L. Nipissing

Ottawa

St. John R.

Saint John

Halifax

Minneapolis

Lake Michigan

L. Simcoe

Kingston

Lake Huron

Toronto

Mississauga

Hamilton

L. Ontario

Bay of Fundy

Yarmouth

Boston

Detroit

London

Windsor

Buffalo

Lake Erie

Niagara Falls

Mississippi R.

Chicago

New York City

N E W S

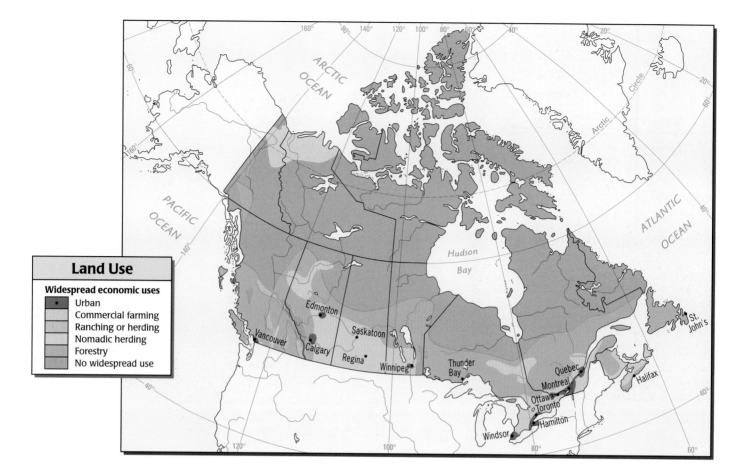

Land Use

Widespread economic uses
- Urban
- Commercial farming
- Ranching or herding
- Nomadic herding
- Forestry
- No widespread use

Focus on Canada's Resources

- Natural resources—minerals, forests, rich soils—are keys to the Canadian economy.
- Each year Canada mines more than 15 times as much iron ore as all other minerals combined.
- Nearly a third of its forest products comes from British Columbia.

Wheat Exports

80%

Total Produced

Mineral Production

Other minerals*
Lead
Nickel
Copper
Zinc

Iron ore
30 million metric tons

*Uranium, Molybdenum, Silver, Gold

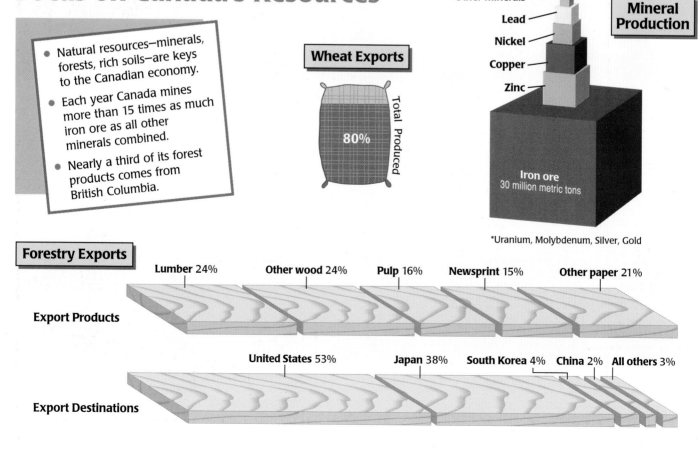

Forestry Exports

Export Products

Lumber 24%   Other wood 24%   Pulp 16%   Newsprint 15%   Other paper 21%

Export Destinations

United States 53%   Japan 38%   South Korea 4%   China 2%   All others 3%

Toronto's landmarks include the CN Tower and the SkyDome. Can you find the CN Tower in the cross section of the Great Lakes on pages 28–29?

Major Highways

— Trans-Canada and other major highways

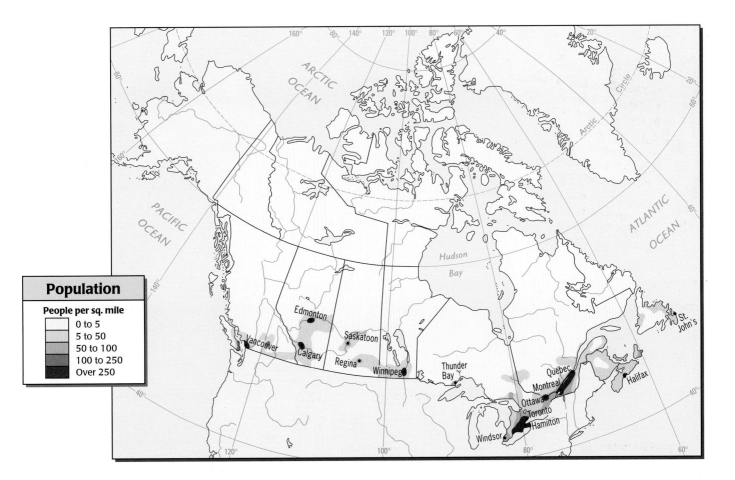

Population

People per sq. mile

	0 to 5
	5 to 50
	50 to 100
	100 to 250
	Over 250

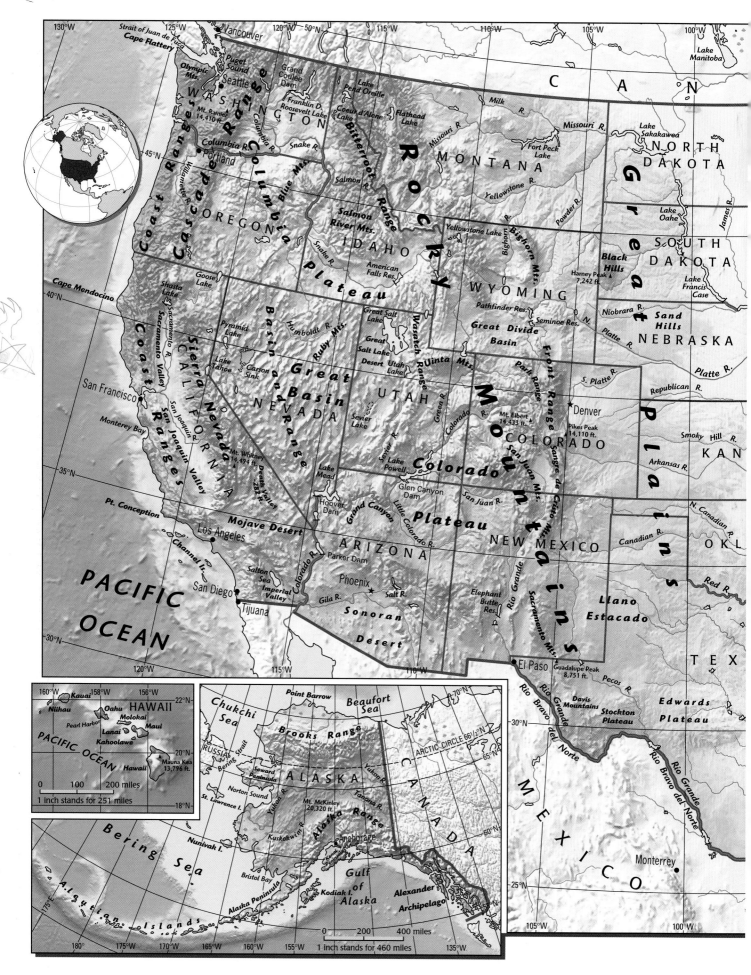

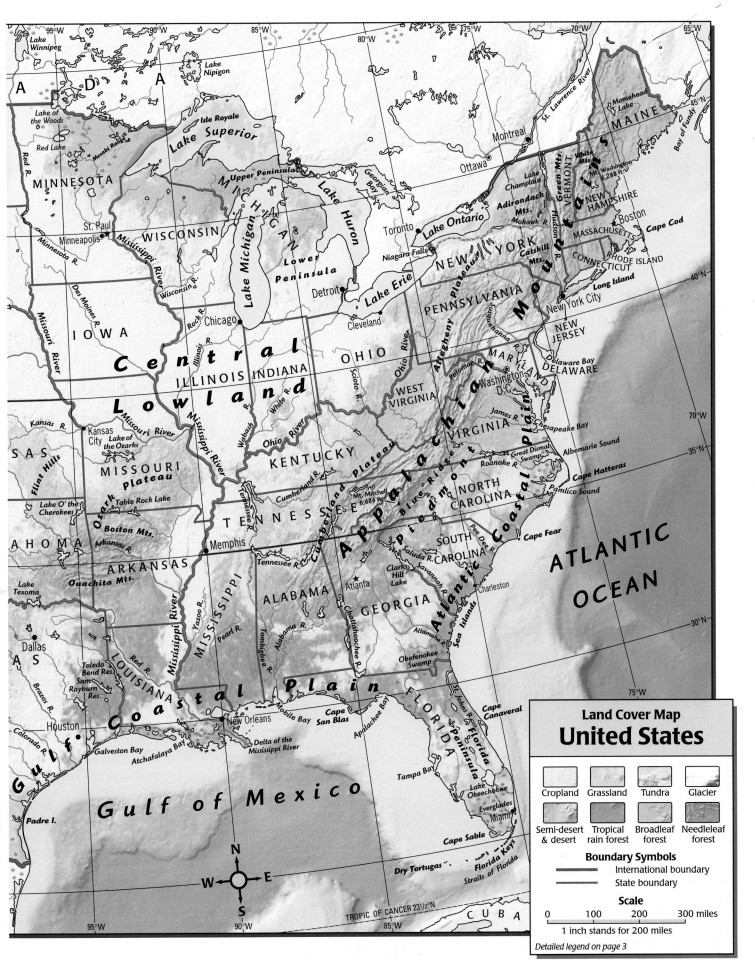

Cropland Grassland Tundra Glacier

Semi-desert & desert Tropical rain forest Broadleaf forest Needleleaf forest

Boundary Symbols

International boundary

State boundary

Scale

0   100   200   300 miles

1 inch stands for 200 miles

Detailed legend on page 3

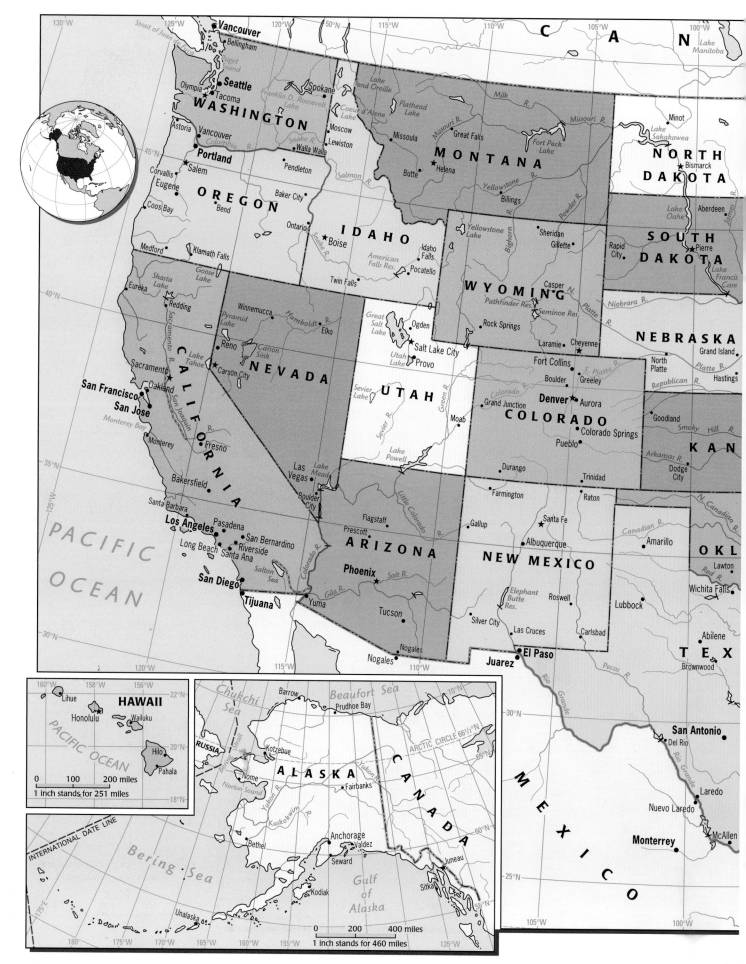

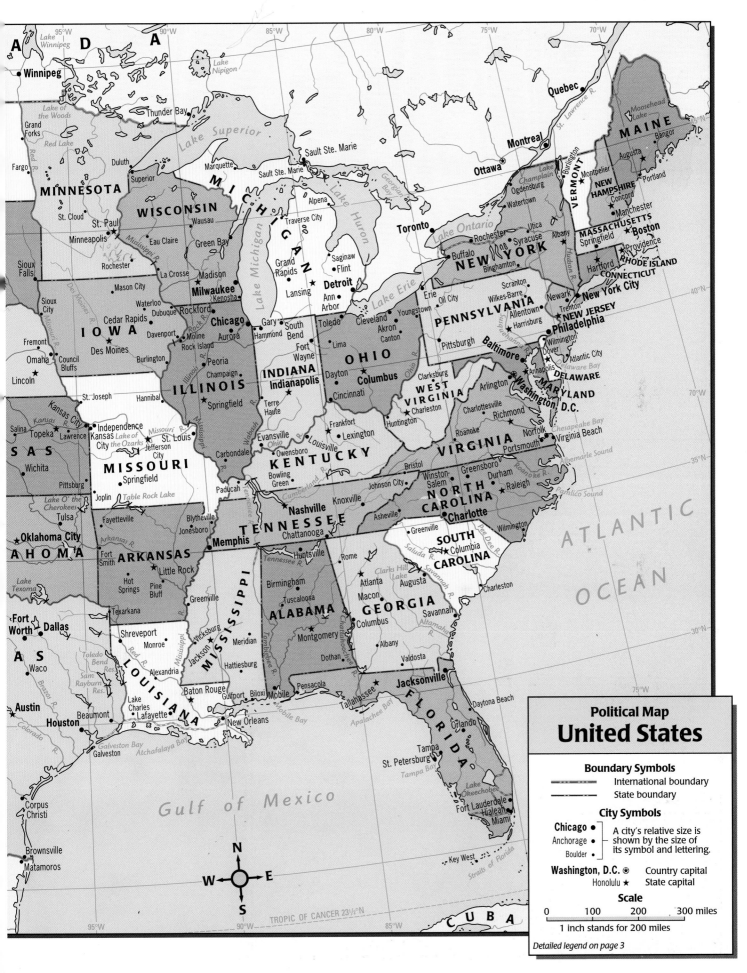

Political Map

United States

Boundary Symbols
— ·· — ·· — International boundary
———— State boundary

City Symbols
Chicago ● — A city's relative size is
Anchorage ● — shown by the size of
Boulder ● — its symbol and lettering.

Washington, D.C. ⊛ — Country capital
Honolulu ★ — State capital

Scale
0   100   200   300 miles
1 inch stands for 200 miles

Detailed legend on page 3

Elevation Map
United States

Feet Above Sea Level

Over 10,000
5,000 to 10,000
2,000 to 5,000
1,000 to 2,000
500 to 1,000
0 to 500
Below sea level

Water Depth in Feet

Less than 600
Greater than 600

Boundary Symbols

International boundary
State boundary

Scale

0   100   200   300 miles

1 inch stands for 200 miles

Detailed legend on page 4

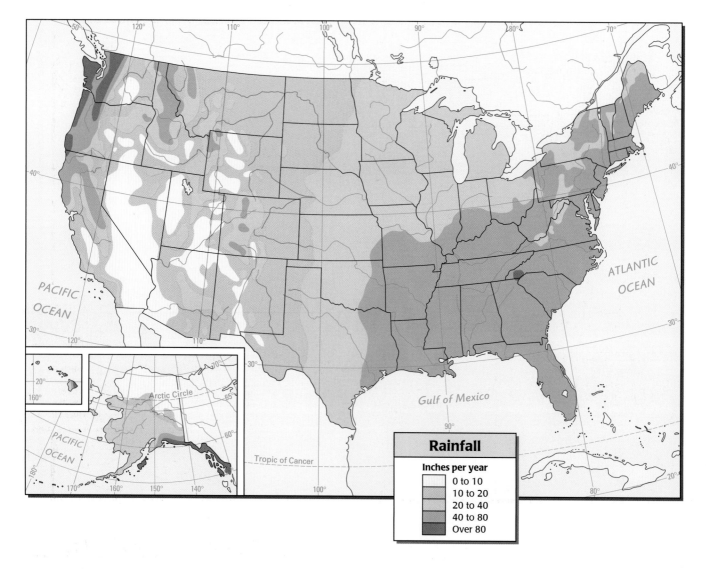

Rainfall

Inches per year

- 0 to 10
- 10 to 20
- 20 to 40
- 40 to 80
- Over 80

Snow blankets Mt. Hood, Oregon. Ten inches of snow are counted as one inch of rain.

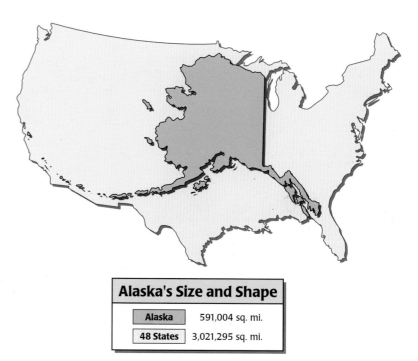

Alaska's Size and Shape

Alaska	591,004 sq. mi.
48 States	3,021,295 sq. mi.

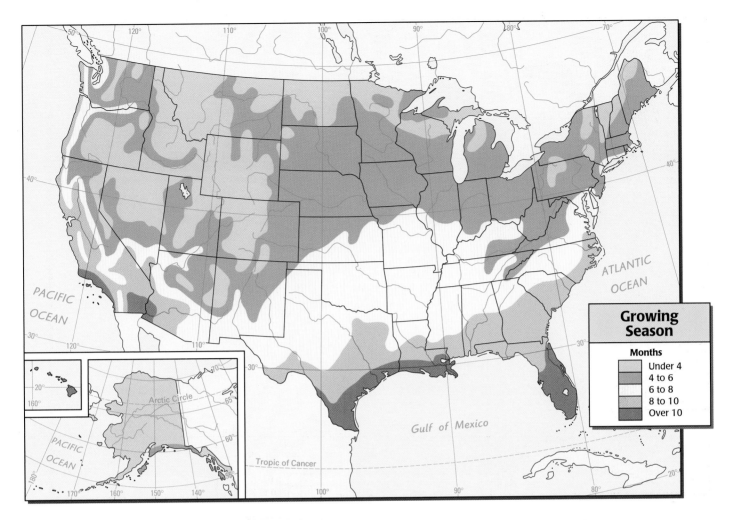

Growing Season

Months
- Under 4
- 4 to 6
- 6 to 8
- 8 to 10
- Over 10

Focus on Regions of the United States

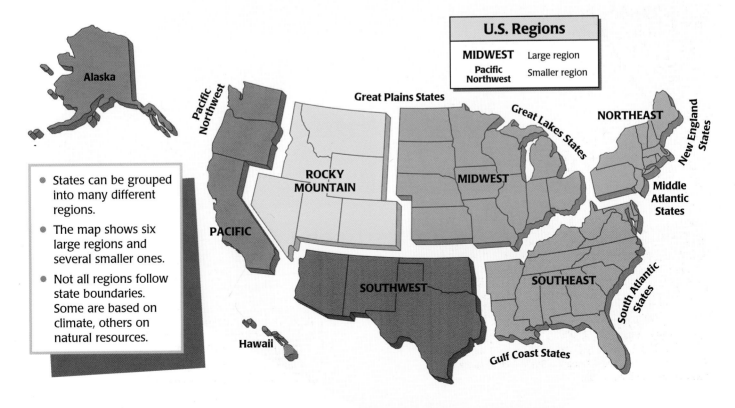

U.S. Regions

MIDWEST	Large region
Pacific Northwest	Smaller region

- States can be grouped into many different regions.
- The map shows six large regions and several smaller ones.
- Not all regions follow state boundaries. Some are based on climate, others on natural resources.

Alaska

Hawaii

Pacific Northwest

ROCKY MOUNTAIN

PACIFIC

SOUTHWEST

Great Plains States

MIDWEST

Great Lakes States

NORTHEAST

New England States

Middle Atlantic States

SOUTHEAST

South Atlantic States

Gulf Coast States

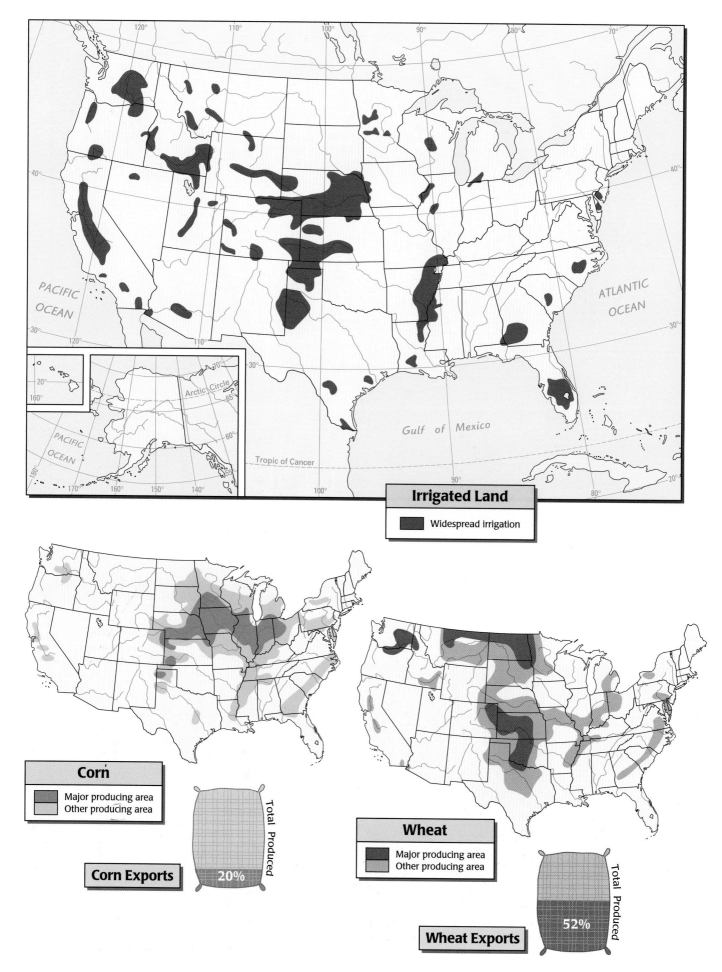

Irrigated Land

Widespread irrigation

PACIFIC OCEAN

ATLANTIC OCEAN

Gulf of Mexico

Tropic of Cancer

Arctic Circle

PACIFIC OCEAN

Corn

Major producing area
Other producing area

Corn Exports

Total Produced

20%

Wheat

Major producing area
Other producing area

Wheat Exports

Total Produced

52%

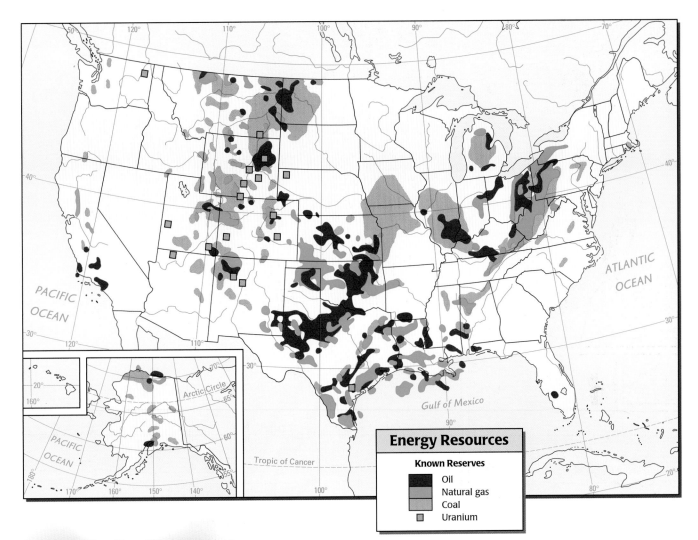

Energy Resources

Known Reserves

- Oil
- Natural gas
- Coal
- Uranium

Who Needs Oil to Grow Wheat?

We do. In much of the world, farm work relies on muscle power. But here farming relies on energy resources. What are some of the ways farms use energy?

Farmers conserve soil by alternating crops and by plowing curved fields that follow the natural slope of the land. Their crops may be used to make *ethanol*, an alternative fuel that helps conserve oil.

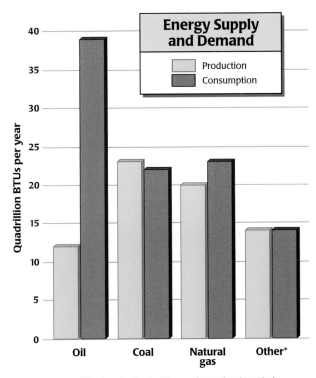

Energy Supply and Demand

- Production
- Consumption

Quadrillion BTUs per year

Oil   Coal   Natural gas   Other*

*Nuclear, hydroelectric, geothermal, solar, wind

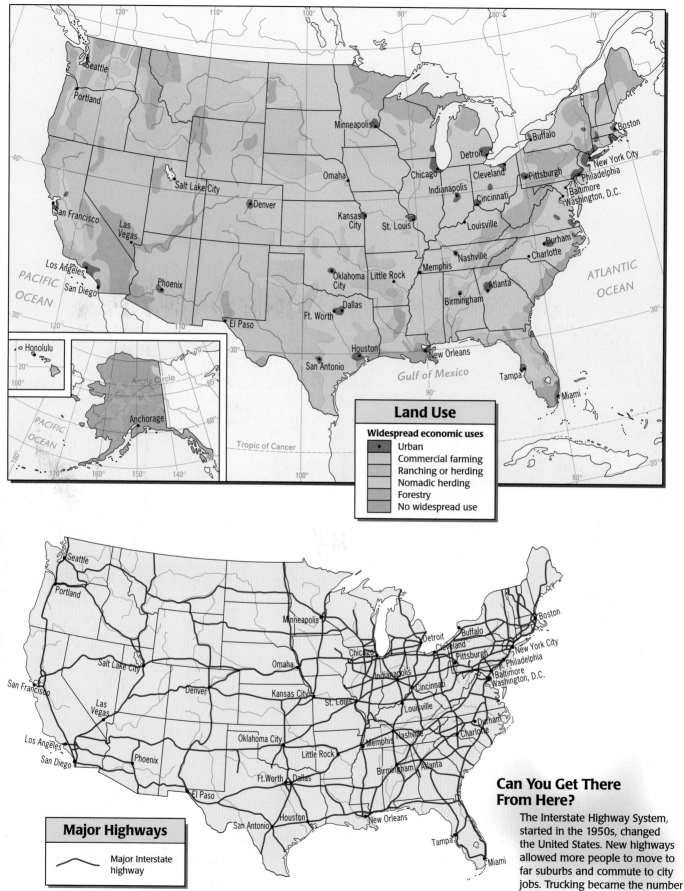

Land Use

Widespread economic uses
- Urban
- Commercial farming
- Ranching or herding
- Nomadic herding
- Forestry
- No widespread use

Major Highways

Major Interstate highway

Can You Get There From Here?

The Interstate Highway System, started in the 1950s, changed the United States. New highways allowed more people to move to far suburbs and commute to city jobs. Trucking became the number one way of moving goods.

Focus on Where Americans Live

New Yorkers enjoy a sunny day in Central Park. Despite limited space for growth, New York is the largest city in the United States.

- In 1790 only 5% of Americans lived in cities. Since then the country has become more and more urban.
- The East Coast was colonized first, and the East Coast states still have more people than the West Coast states.
- Today the fastest-growing cities are in the South and West.

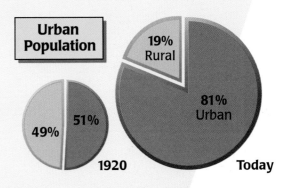

Urban Population

49% 51%
1920

19% Rural
81% Urban
Today

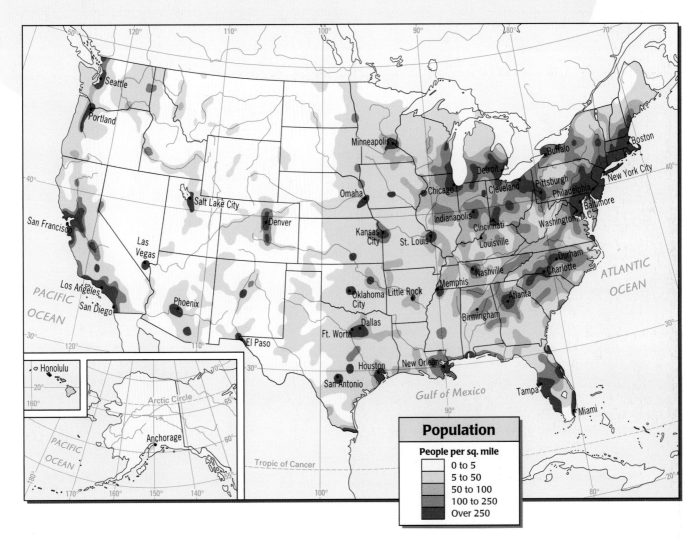

Population

People per sq. mile

	0 to 5
	5 to 50
	50 to 100
	100 to 250
	Over 250

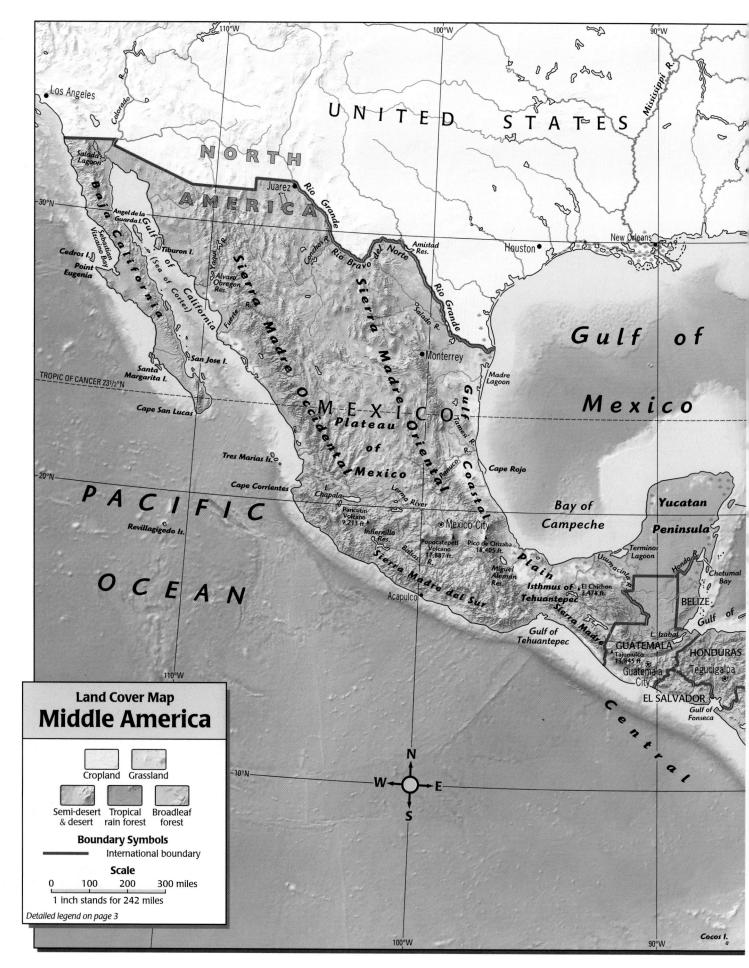

UNITED STATES

NORTH AMERICA

Los Angeles

Colorado

Baja California

Gulf of California (Sea of Cortes)

Salada Lagoon

Angel de la Guarda I.

Sebastian Vizcaino Bay

Cedros I.

Point Eugenia

Tiburon I.

Santa Margarita I.

San Jose I.

Alvaro Obregon Res.

Yaqui R.

Fuerte R.

Juarez

Rio Grande

Conchos R.

Rio Bravo del Norte

Amistad Res.

Salado R.

Rio Grande

Monterrey

Madre Lagoon

Sierra Madre Occidental

Sierra Madre Oriental

MEXICO

Plateau of Mexico

Gulf of Mexico

Gulf of Campeche

New Orleans

Houston

Gulf Coastal

Cape Rojo

Tres Marias Is.

Cape Corrientes

L. Chapala

Lerma River

Panuco R.

Paricutin Volcano 9,213 ft.

Infiernillo Res.

Balsas R.

Mexico City

Popocatepetl Volcano 17,887 ft.

Pico de Orizaba 18,405 ft.

Miguel Aleman Res.

Isthmus of Tehuantepec

El Chichon 3,478 ft.

Plain

Yucatan Peninsula

Terminos Lagoon

Usumacinta R.

Hondo R.

Chetumal Bay

BELIZE

Gulf of

L. Izabal

GUATEMALA

Tajumulco 13,845 ft.

Guatemala City

Sierra Madre

HONDURAS

Tegucigalpa

EL SALVADOR

Gulf of Fonseca

Central

Sierra Madre del Sur

Acapulco

Gulf of Tehuantepec

PACIFIC OCEAN

Revillagigedo Is.

Cocos I.

Bay of Campeche

TROPIC OF CANCER 23½°N

Cape San Lucas

Mississippi R.

30°N

20°N

10°N

110°W

100°W

90°W

N W E S

Land Cover Map
Middle America

Cropland   Grassland

Semi-desert & desert   Tropical rain forest   Broadleaf forest

Boundary Symbols

International boundary

Scale

0   100   200   300 miles

1 inch stands for 242 miles

Detailed legend on page 3

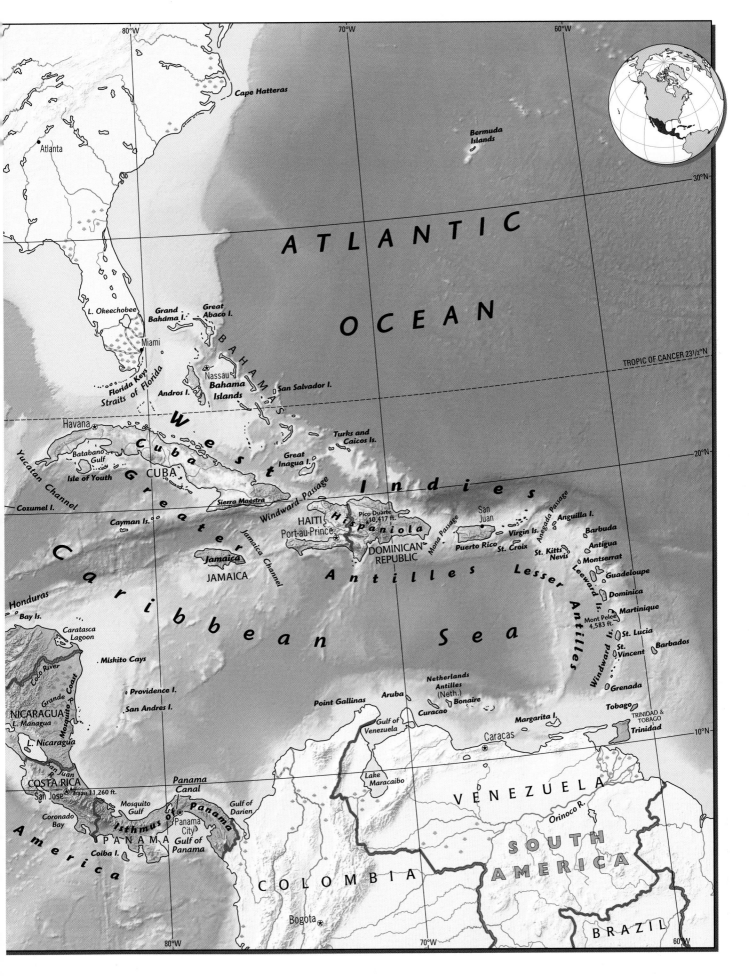

ATLANTIC

OCEAN

Atlanta

Cape Hatteras

Bermuda
Islands

30°N

L. Okeechobee
Grand
Bahdma I.
Great
Abaco I.

Miami

B
A
H
A
M
A
S

TROPIC OF CANCER 23½°N

Florida Keys
Straits of Florida

Nassau

Bahama
Islands

San Salvador I.

Andros I.

Havana

Cuba

W
e
s
t

20°N

Batabano
Gulf

Isle of Youth

CUBA

G
r
e
a
t
e
r

Turks and
Caicos Is.

Great
Inagua I.

I
n
d
i
e
s

Yucatan Channel

Cozumel I.

Cayman Is.

Sierra Maestra

Windward Passage

HAITI
Port-au-Prince

Hispaniola

Pico Duarte
10,417 ft.

San
Juan

Anegada Passage

Anguilla I.

Mona Passage

Puerto Rico

St. Croix

Virgin Is.

Barbuda

Antigua

St. Kitts
Nevis

Montserrat

Leeward Is.

Guadeloupe

C
a
r
i
b
b
e
a
n

Jamaica

JAMAICA

Jamaica Channel

DOMINICAN
REPUBLIC

A
n
t
i
l
l
e
s

L
e
s
s
e
r

A
n
t
i
l
l
e
s

Dominica

Mont Pelee
4,583 ft.

Martinique

Honduras

Bay Is.

Caratasca
Lagoon

Miskito Cays

S
e
a

W
i
n
d
w
a
r
d

I
s
.

St.
Vincent

St. Lucia

Barbados

Coco River

Grande R.

Mosquito Coast

Providence I.

San Andres I.

Netherlands
Antilles
(Neth.)

Aruba

Point Gallinas

Bonaire

Curacao

Grenada

Margarita I.

Tobago

TRINIDAD &
TOBAGO

NICARAGUA

L. Managua

L. Nicaragua

San
Juan
R.

Gulf of
Venezuela

Caracas

Trinidad

10°N

COSTA RICA

San Jose

Irazu 11,260 ft.

Panama
Canal

Mosquito
Gulf

Coronado
Bay

A
m
e
r
i
c
a

Coiba I.

Isthmus of Panama

Panama
City

PANAMA

Gulf of
Panama

Gulf of
Darien

Lake
Maracaibo

VENEZUELA

Orinoco R.

SOUTH

AMERICA

COLOMBIA

Bogota

BRAZIL

80°W

70°W

60°W

Political Map
Middle America

Boundary Symbols
— · — · — International boundary
———— State boundary

City Symbols
Tijuana •
Ponce •
Limon •

A city's relative size is shown by the size of its symbol and lettering.

Havana ⊛ National capital

Scale
0   100   200   300 miles

1 inch stands for 242 miles

Detailed legend on page 3

Mexican States not named on map

1 AGUASCALIENTES
2 GUANAJUATO
3 QUERETARO
4 HIDALGO
5 MEXICO
6 FEDERAL DISTRICT
7 MORELOS
8 TLAXCALA

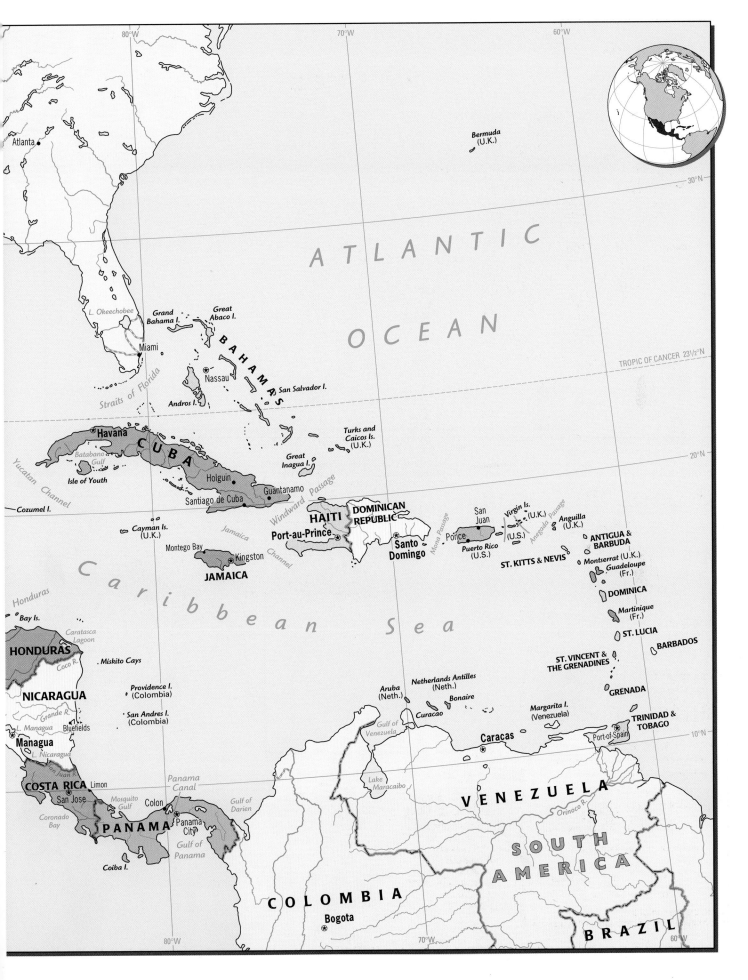

ATLANTIC

OCEAN

Caribbean Sea

Atlanta

L. Okeechobee

Grand Bahama I.
Great Abaco I.
Miami
BAHAMAS
Nassau
San Salvador I.
Andros I.
Straits of Florida

Bermuda
(U.K.)

TROPIC OF CANCER 23½°N

Havana
CUBA
Batabano Gulf
Isle of Youth
Holguin
Santiago de Cuba
Guantanamo
Yucatan Channel
Cozumel I.

Turks and
Caicos Is.
(U.K.)

Great
Inagua I.

Windward Passage

HAITI
Port-au-Prince
DOMINICAN
REPUBLIC
Santo
Domingo

Mona Passage
San
Juan
Ponce
Puerto Rico
(U.S.)

Virgin Is.
(U.K.)
(U.S.)
Anegada Passage
Anguilla
(U.K.)

ANTIGUA &
BARBUDA
Montserrat (U.K.)
Guadeloupe
(Fr.)

ST. KITTS & NEVIS

DOMINICA

Martinique
(Fr.)

Cayman Is.
(U.K.)
Jamaica
Montego Bay
Kingston
JAMAICA

Jamaica Channel

ST. LUCIA

BARBADOS

ST. VINCENT &
THE GRENADINES

GRENADA

Honduras
Bay Is.
Caratasca
Lagoon
HONDURAS
Coco R.
Miskito Cays

NICARAGUA
Grande R.
L. Managua
Bluefields
Managua
L. Nicaragua

Providence I.
(Colombia)

San Andres I.
(Colombia)

Aruba
(Neth.)
Curacao
Gulf of
Venezuela

Netherlands Antilles
(Neth.)
Bonaire

Margarita I.
(Venezuela)

Caracas

TRINIDAD &
TOBAGO
Port-of-Spain

COSTA RICA
Limon
San Jose
San Juan R.
Mosquito Gulf
Colon
Coronado Bay
PANAMA
Panama
City
Coiba I.

Panama
Canal
Gulf of
Darien
Gulf of
Panama

Lake
Maracaibo
VENEZUELA
Orinoco R.

SOUTH
AMERICA

COLOMBIA
Bogota

BRAZIL

80°W

70°W

60°W

30°N

20°N

10°N

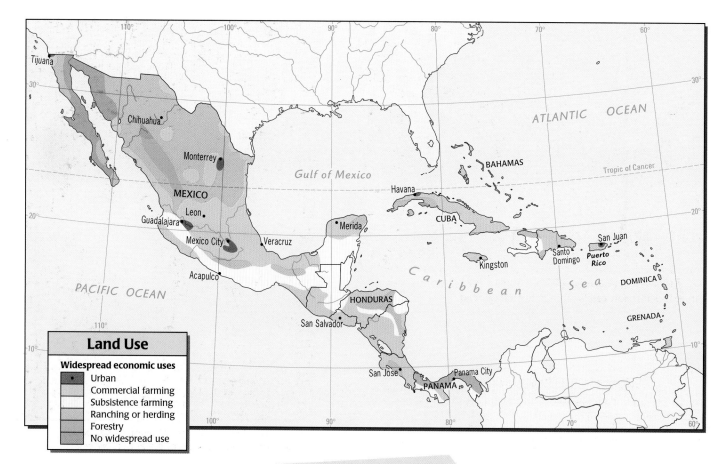

Land Use

Widespread economic uses
- Urban
- Commercial farming
- Subsistence farming
- Ranching or herding
- Forestry
- No widespread use

Focus on the Panama Canal

- Most ships traveling between Atlantic and Pacific ports pass through the Panama Canal.
- The canal saves them thousands of miles and several days.
- Its narrowness makes the canal a potential "choke point."

Water-filled chambers called *locks* raise and lower ships from one level to another.

Schoolchildren in Havana reflect Cuba's racial diversity. An old Spanish fort can be seen in the background.

Mexico City's Roman Catholic cathedral stands beside the ruins of the main temple of the ancient Aztecs.

Where Is Rio Bravo del Norte?

It's called the Rio Grande on the U.S. side of the border, but in Mexico it's Rio Bravo del Norte—two Spanish names for the same river.

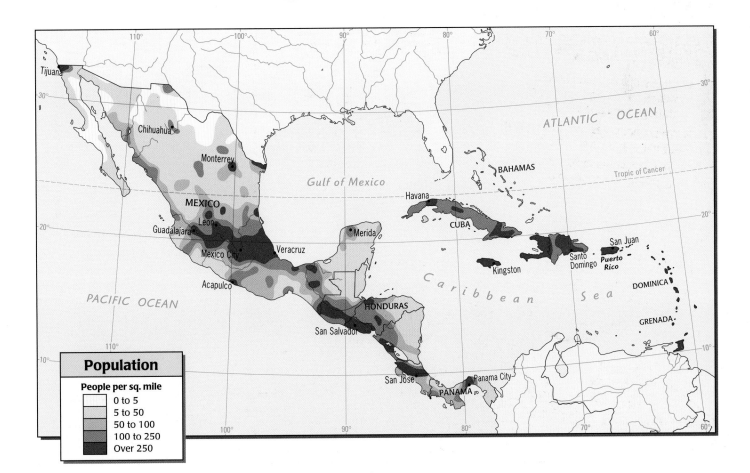

Population

People per sq. mile

- 0 to 5
- 5 to 50
- 50 to 100
- 100 to 250
- Over 250

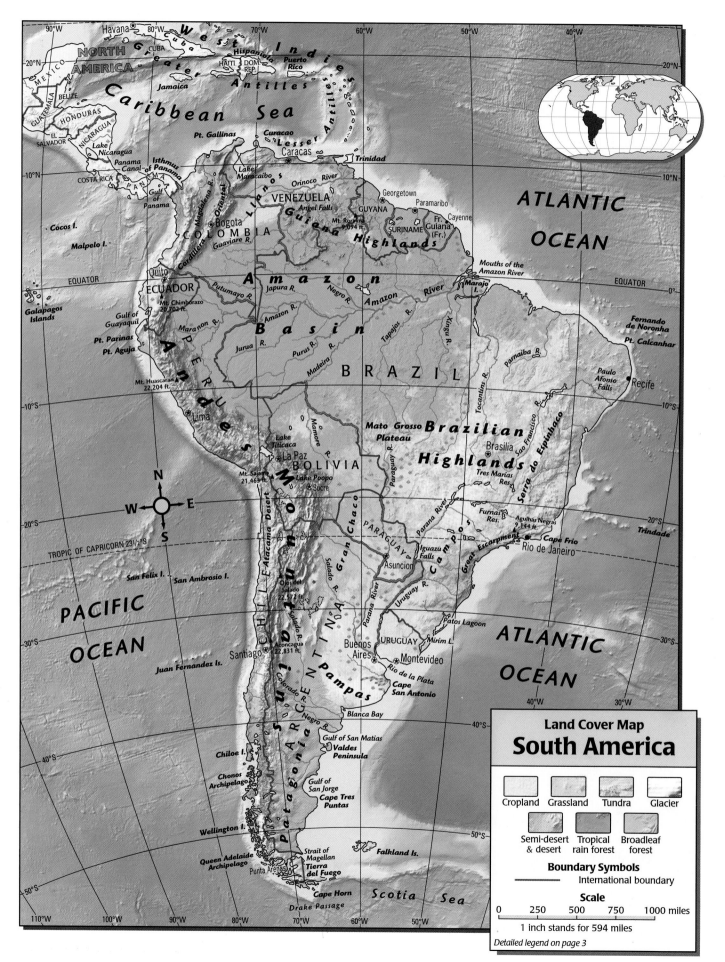

North America

Mexico
Guatemala
Belize
Honduras
El Salvador
Nicaragua
Costa Rica
Panama

Havana
Cuba
Jamaica
Hispaniola
HAITI
DOM. REP.
Puerto Rico
West Indies
Greater Antilles
Lesser Antilles
Curacao
Trinidad
Caribbean Sea
Pt. Gallinas

Cocos I.
Malpelo I.
Isthmus of Panama
Panama Canal
Gulf of Panama

VENEZUELA
Caracas
Lake Maracaibo
Bogota
COLOMBIA
Orinoco River
Llanos
Angel Falls
Mt. Roraima 9,094 ft.
GUYANA
Georgetown
Paramaribo
SURINAME
Cayenne
Fr. Guiana (Fr.)
Guiana Highlands

ATLANTIC OCEAN

Quito
ECUADOR
Mt. Chimborazo 20,702 ft.
Gulf of Guayaquil
Pt. Parinas
Pt. Aguja
Galapagos Islands
EQUATOR

Putumayo R.
Japura R.
Negro R.
Amazon River
Marajo I.
Mouths of the Amazon River

Amazon Basin
Amazon R.
Jurua R.
Purus R.
Madeira R.
Tapajos R.
Xingu R.
Parnaiba R.

Fernando de Noronha
Pt. Calcanhar

Maranon R.

Mt. Huascaran 22,204 ft.
Lima

B R A Z I L

Paulo Afonso Falls
Recife

A n d e s

Lake Titicaca
La Paz
BOLIVIA
Sucre
Lake Poopo
Mt. Sajama 21,463 ft.

Mamore R.

Mato Grosso Plateau

Brazilian Highlands
Brasilia
Tocantins R.
Sao Francisco R.
Serra do Espinhaco

Tres Marias Res.

N
W E
S

M o u n t a i n s

Salado R.

Paraguay R.

Furnas Res.
Campos
Agulhas Negras 9,144 ft.

TROPIC OF CAPRICORN 23½°S

Atacama Desert

Gran Chaco
PARAGUAY
Asuncion

Parana River
Iguazu Falls
Great Escarpment

Cape Frio
Rio de Janeiro

Trindade

San Felix I.
San Ambrosio I.

Ojos del Salado 22,572 ft.

Salado R.

Uruguay R.

PACIFIC OCEAN

CHILE
ARGENTINA
Aconcagua 22,831 ft.
Santiago

Parana River
Pampas

Juan Fernandez Is.

Salado R.

Buenos Aires
URUGUAY
Patos Lagoon
Mirim L.
Montevideo

ATLANTIC OCEAN

Colorado R.

Rio de la Plata
Cape San Antonio

Negro R.

Blanca Bay
Gulf of San Matias
Valdes Peninsula

Chiloe I.
Chonos Archipelago
Gulf of San Jorge
Cape Tres Puntas

Patagonia

Wellington I.

Queen Adelaide Archipelago
Punta Arenas
Strait of Magellan
Tierra del Fuego
Falkland Is.

Cape Horn
Drake Passage
Scotia Sea

Land Cover Map
South America

Cropland	Grassland	Tundra	Glacier

Semi-desert & desert	Tropical rain forest	Broadleaf forest

Boundary Symbols
——— International boundary

Scale
0   250   500   750   1000 miles
1 inch stands for 594 miles
Detailed legend on page 3

Havana
NORTH
AMERICA
MEXICO
CUBA
HAITI
DOM.
REP.
Puerto Rico
(U.S.)
Anguilla (U.K.)
ANTIGUA & BARBUDA
Guadeloupe (Fr.)
DOMINICA
Martinique (Fr.)
ST. LUCIA
BARBADOS
GRENADA
TRINIDAD & TOBAGO
ST. KITTS & NEVIS
ST. VINCENT &
THE GRENADINES
Curacao
(Neth.)
JAMAICA
BELIZE
GUATEMALA
HONDURAS
EL
SALVADOR
NICARAGUA
Lake
Nicaragua
COSTA RICA
PANAMA
Panama
Canal

Caribbean Sea

Cocos I.
(Costa Rica)

Malpelo I.
(Colombia)

Barranquilla
Maracaibo
Caracas
Barquisimeto
Lake
Maracaibo
Orinoco River
Ciudad Guyana
Georgetown
Paramaribo
Cayenne
VENEZUELA
GUYANA
SURINAME
Fr.
Guiana
(Fr.)
Medellin
Bucaramanga
Angel Falls
Bogota
COLOMBIA
Cali
Magdalena
Guaviare R.
Boa Vista
Macapa
Mouths of
the Amazon
Quito
ECUADOR
Guayaquil
Gulf of
Guayaquil
Iquitos
Putumayo R.
Japura R.
Negro
Amazon River
Manaus
Santarem
Belem
Sao Luis
Fernando
de Noronha
(Brazil)

Galapagos
Islands
(Ecuador)

EQUATOR

Piura
Maranon
Jurua R.
Amazon River
Puru R.
Madeira R.
BRAZIL
Fortaleza
Teresina
Natal
Joao Pessoa
Recife
Maceio
Chiclayo
Trujillo
PERU
Rio
Branco
Porto Velho
Tapajos R.
Xingu R.
Tocantins R.
Parnaiba R.
Paulo
Afonso
Falls
Feira de
Santana
Aracaju
Salvador
Lima
Callao
Huancayo
Cusco
Lake
Titicaca
La Paz
BOLIVIA
Santa Cruz
Sucre
Potosi
Cuiaba
Brasilia
Goiania
Montes Claros
Uberaba
Belo Horizonte
Tres Marias
Res.
Sao Francisco R.
Mamore R.
Campo
Grande
Furnas
Res.
Vitoria
Campos
Campinas
Arequipa
Iquique
Lake
Poopo
PARAGUAY
Paraguay R.
Parana R.
Sao Paulo
Rio de Janeiro
Santos
Trindade
(Brazil)
Antofagasta
Salta
Tucuman
Asuncion
Iguazu
Falls
Curitiba
Resistencia
Salado R.
Florianopolis
Santa
Maria
Porto Alegre
Santiago
del Estero
Uruguay R.
La Serena
CHILE
San
Juan
Cordoba
Santa Fe
Salto
URUGUAY
Patos Lagoon
Vina del Mar
Valparaiso
Santiago
San Luis
Rosario
Buenos Aires
San Justo
Montevideo
Mirim L.
Rio de la Plata
La Plata
Juan Fernandez Is.
(Chile)
ARGENTINA
Colorado R.
Mar del Plata
San Felix I.
(Chile)
San Ambrosio I.
(Chile)
Concepcion
Temuco
Negro R.
Bahia Blanca
Blanca Bay
Viedma
Gulf of San Matias
Puerto Montt
Comodoro
Rivadavia
Gulf of
San Jorge
Falkland Is.
(U.K.)
Rio Gallegos
Strait of
Magellan
Punta Arenas
Scotia Sea
Drake Passage

N
W   E
S

TROPIC OF CAPRICORN 23½°S
EQUATOR

90°W 80°W 70°W 60°W 50°W 40°W
20°N
10°N
0°
10°S
20°S
30°S
40°S
50°S

ATLANTIC OCEAN
PACIFIC OCEAN

Political Map
South America

Boundary Symbols
International boundary

City Symbols

Sao Paulo •
Tucuman •
Cusco •

A city's relative size is
shown by the size of
its symbol and lettering.

Caracas ⊛   National capital

Scale

0   250   500   750   1000 miles

1 inch stands for 594 miles

Detailed legend on page 3

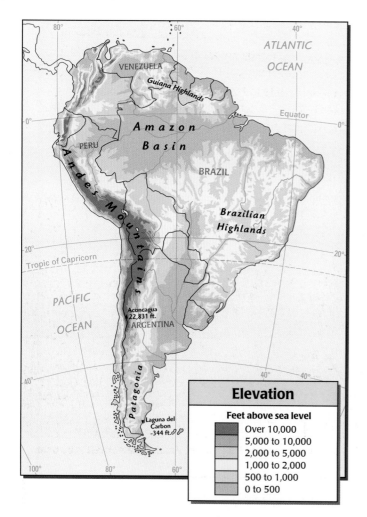

Elevation

Feet above sea level

- Over 10,000
- 5,000 to 10,000
- 2,000 to 5,000
- 1,000 to 2,000
- 500 to 1,000
- 0 to 500

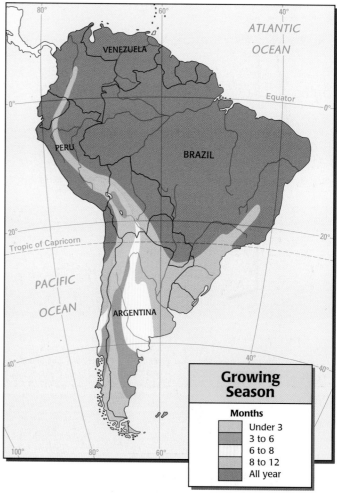

Growing Season

Months

- Under 3
- 3 to 6
- 6 to 8
- 8 to 12
- All year

A Chilean worker trims grapevines. Chile is the world's largest exporter of grapes.

Snow in July?

Seasons occur at opposite times of the year in the Southern and Northern Hemispheres. In Argentina, summer begins in December and snow falls in July and August.

Area Shown

Elevation
Cross Section

Feet above sea level

- Over 10,000
- 5,000 to 10,000
- 2,000 to 5,000
- 1,000 to 2,000
- 500 to 1,000
- 0 to 500

Focus on the Amazon Rain Forest

- Tropical rain forests are an important source of rare plants and the oxygen we breathe.
- The Amazon Rain Forest, the largest in the world, is shrinking.
- Large areas have been *deforested*, cleared for farming and mining.

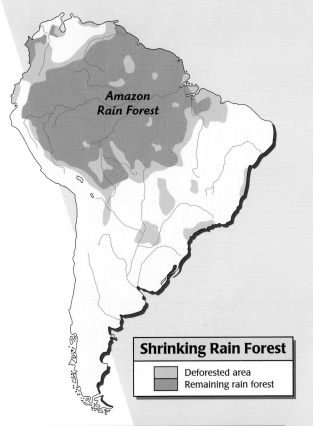

Amazon Rain Forest

Shrinking Rain Forest

	Deforested area
	Remaining rain forest

The easiest way to travel in the dense Amazon Rain Forest is by boat.

In sharp contrast to the Amazon Basin, the Atacama Desert sometimes goes for years without rain.

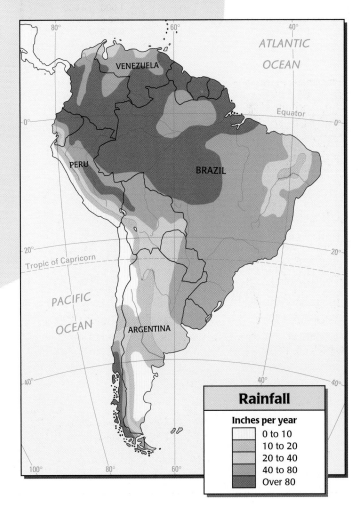

ATLANTIC OCEAN

VENEZUELA

Equator

PERU

BRAZIL

Tropic of Capricorn

PACIFIC OCEAN

ARGENTINA

Rainfall

Inches per year

	0 to 10
	10 to 20
	20 to 40
	40 to 80
	Over 80

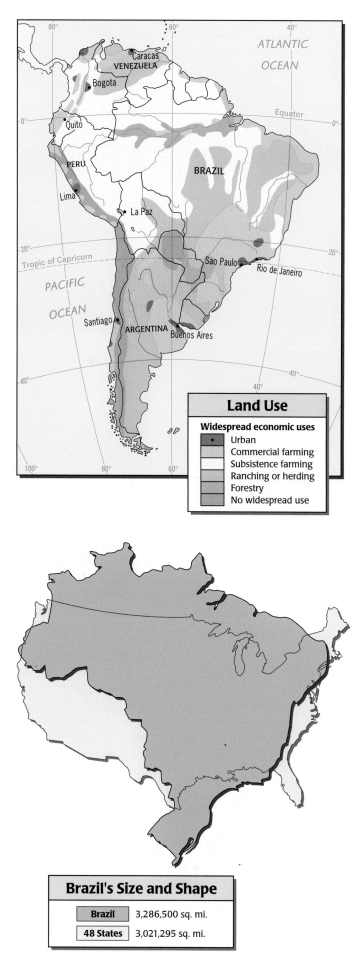

Land Use

Widespread economic uses

•	Urban
	Commercial farming
	Subsistence farming
	Ranching or herding
	Forestry
	No widespread use

Brazil's Size and Shape

Brazil	3,286,500 sq. mi.
48 States	3,021,295 sq. mi.

Who Is El Niño?

Every few years, much of the Pacific Ocean turns unusually warm. Peruvian fishermen noticed that the arrival of warm water meant fewer fish. Since it arrived in late December, they named the phenomenon *El Niño*—Spanish for "the Christ Child."

A man in rural Brazil prepares new thatch for his roof using local plants. Many Brazilians live far from any city.

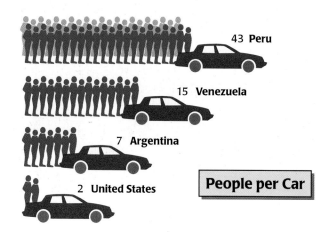

43 **Peru**

15 **Venezuela**

7 **Argentina**

2 **United States**

People per Car

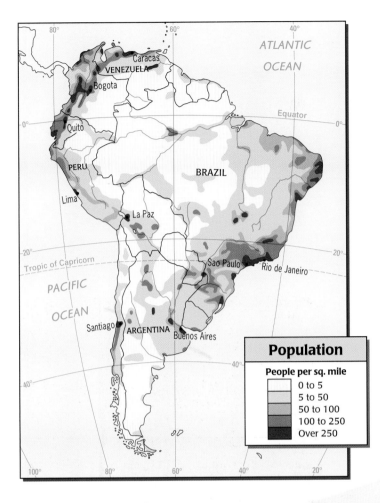

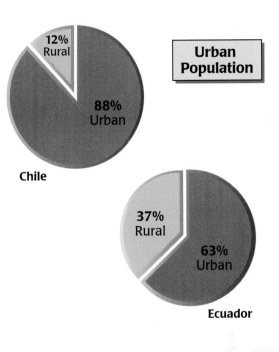

Urban Population

12% Rural

88% Urban

Chile

37% Rural

63% Urban

Ecuador

Focus on Latin America

- The people of South America and Middle America are known as *Latin Americans*.

- Most Latin Americans speak Spanish, Portuguese, or French—languages based on Latin.

- Half of all Latin Americans live in Brazil. Most Brazilians speak Portuguese.

A statue of Christ overlooks the harbor of Rio de Janeiro. Most Latin Americans are Christian.

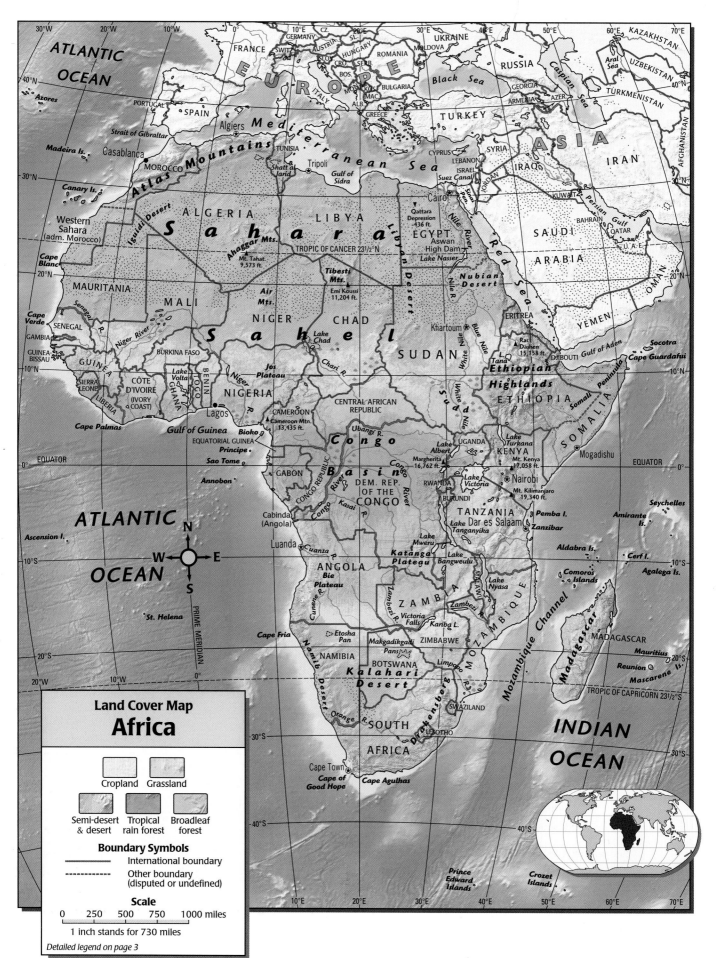

Land Cover Map
Africa

☐ Cropland ☐ Grassland

☐ Semi-desert & desert ☐ Tropical rain forest ☐ Broadleaf forest

Boundary Symbols

——— International boundary

- - - - Other boundary (disputed or undefined)

Scale

0   250   500   750   1000 miles

1 inch stands for 730 miles

Detailed legend on page 3

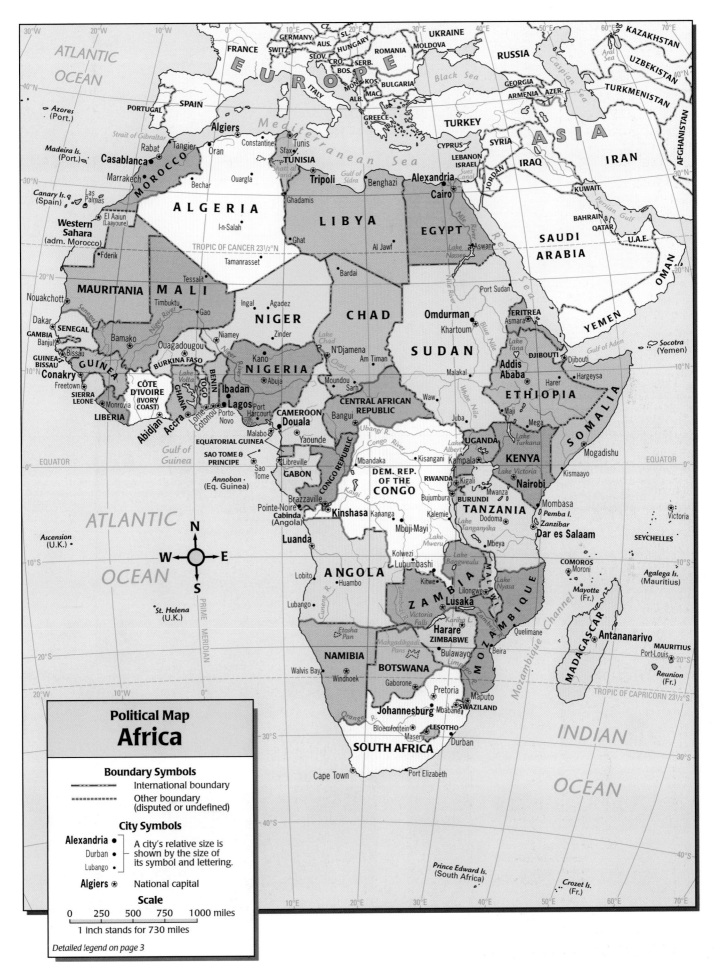

Political Map
Africa

Boundary Symbols
— ·· — ·· —   International boundary
· · · · · · · ·   Other boundary
(disputed or undefined)

City Symbols

Alexandria •
Durban •
Lubango •
A city's relative size is shown by the size of its symbol and lettering.

Algiers ⊛   National capital

Scale
0   250   500   750   1000 miles

1 inch stands for 730 miles

Detailed legend on page 3

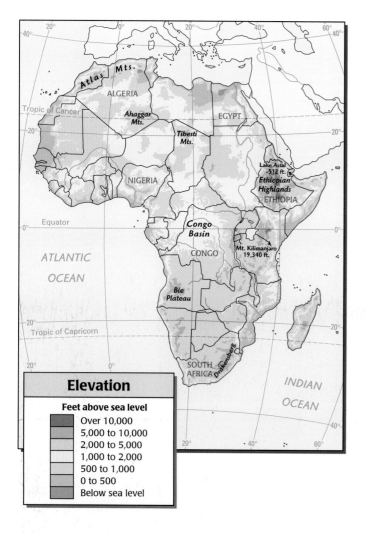

Elevation

Feet above sea level

- Over 10,000
- 5,000 to 10,000
- 2,000 to 5,000
- 1,000 to 2,000
- 500 to 1,000
- 0 to 500
- Below sea level

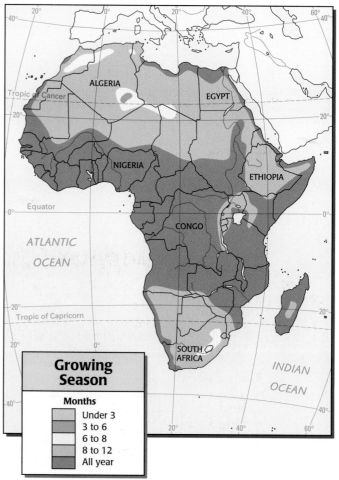

Growing Season

Months

- Under 3
- 3 to 6
- 6 to 8
- 8 to 12
- All year

The Zambezi River drops steeply at Victoria Falls.
African rivers flow from interior plateaus to the coast.

Elephants still roam the savanna near Mt. Kilimanjaro
in one of Tanzania's game preserves.

Focus on the Sahara

- In Arabic, *Sahara* means "desert."
- No other desert is close to its size. The Sahara is larger than the 48 contiguous United States.
- It is famous for sand dunes, but much of the bone-dry Sahara is stony rather than sandy.

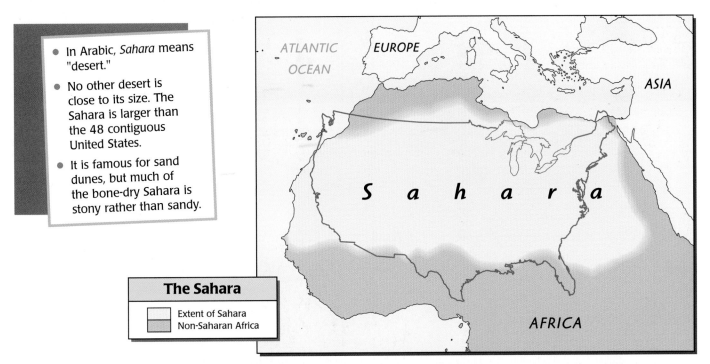

The Sahara

	Extent of Sahara
	Non-Saharan Africa

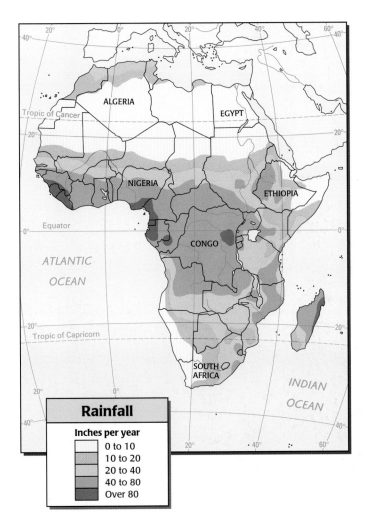

Rainfall

Inches per year

	0 to 10
	10 to 20
	20 to 40
	40 to 80
	Over 80

Ancient Egyptian pyramids tower over the Sahara. For scale, find the cars in the lower left part of the picture.

How Hot Was It?

The hottest temperature on record is 136.4°F. It was measured *in the shade* in the Libyan part of the Sahara. The North American record is 134°F, set in Death Valley, California.

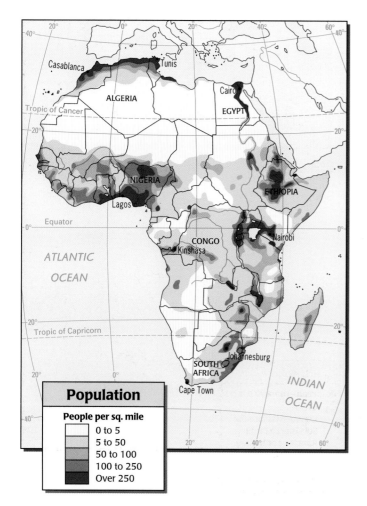

Population

People per sq. mile
- 0 to 5
- 5 to 50
- 50 to 100
- 100 to 250
- Over 250

Say What?

More than 800 languages are spoken in Africa's 53 countries. Communication can be difficult, not just between countries, but within them as well. In many places, the only common language is that of the last colonial power.

Villagers in Niger wear traditional dresses. Most Africans live in small villages.

Focus on Independence in Africa

- Between 1884 and 1940, most of Africa was ruled by European countries.
- From 1941 to 1968, 39 African countries won independence.
- Eleven more African countries gained their independence between 1973 and 1993.

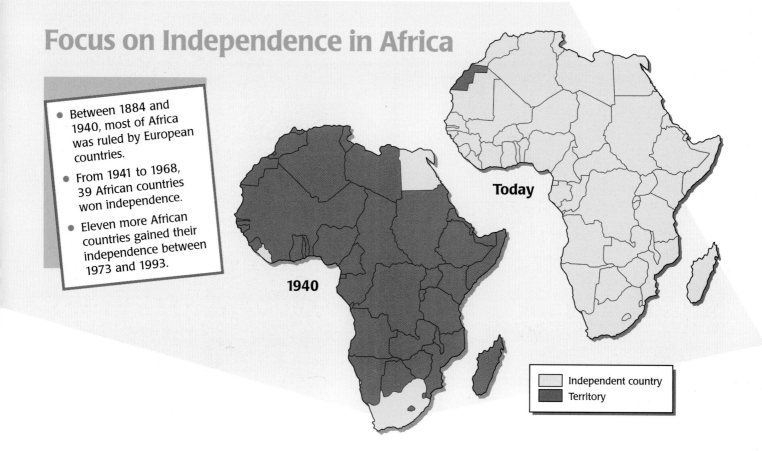

1940

Today

- Independent country
- Territory

In Zimbabwe, a farmer tends her corn crop.
Her house stands nearby.

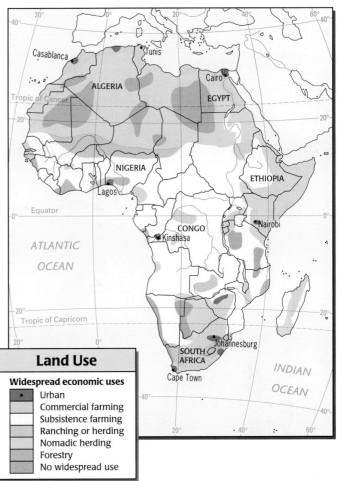

Land Use

Widespread economic uses

- Urban
- Commercial farming
- Subsistence farming
- Ranching or herding
- Nomadic herding
- Forestry
- No widespread use

Kenya's Urban Population

42% Urban

58% Rural

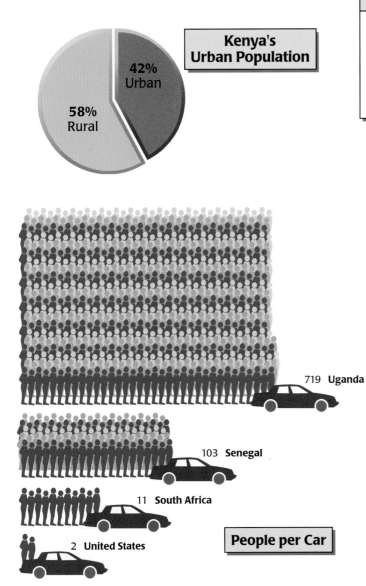

719 **Uganda**

103 **Senegal**

11 **South Africa**

2 **United States**

People per Car

Nairobi is the capital of Kenya and a major business center for East Africa.

Land Cover Map
Europe

Cropland Grassland Tundra Glacier

Semi-desert & desert Broadleaf forest Needleleaf forest

Boundary Symbols
International boundary
Other boundary (disputed or undefined)
Small country

Scale
0   100   200   300   400 miles
1 inch stands for 276 miles

Detailed legend on page 3

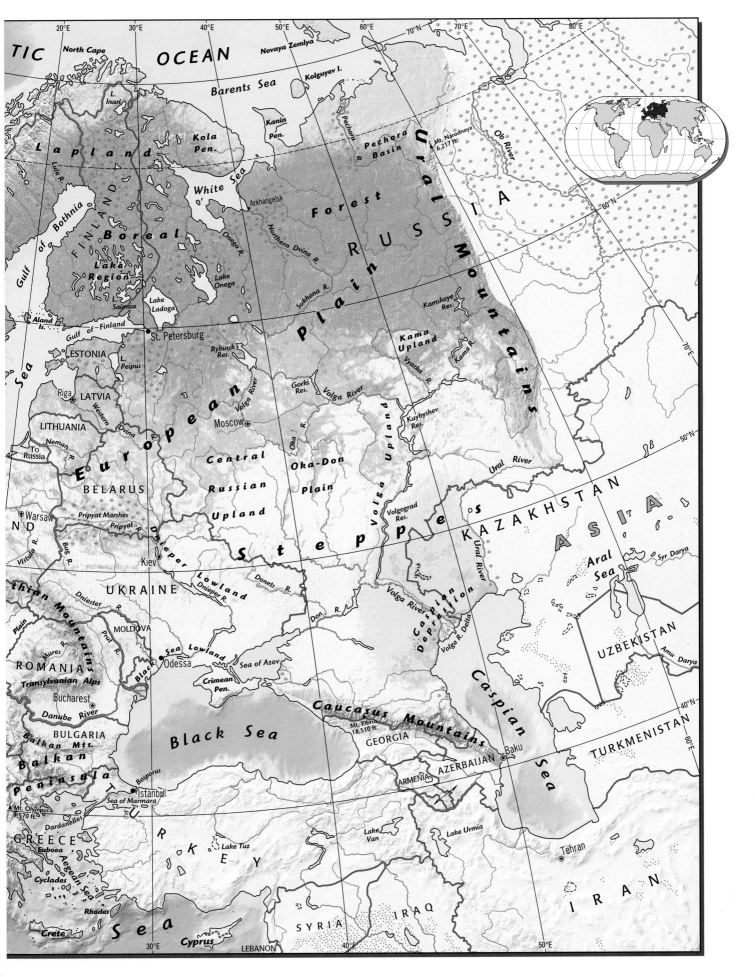

TIC OCEAN

North Cape

Novaya Zemlya

Barents Sea

Kolguyev I.

Kanin Pen.

Pechora R.

Pechora Basin

Ob River

Mt. Narodnaya 6,217 ft.

Lapland

L. Inari

Kola Pen.

White Sea

Arkhangelsk

Forest

Gulf of Bothnia

FINLAND

Boreal

Lake Region

L. Saimaa

Aland Is.

Northern Dvina R.

Onega R.

Lake Onega

Lake Ladoga

Sukhona R.

RUSSIA

U r a l s   M o u n t a i n s

Kamskoye Res.

Kama Upland

Kama R.

Vyatka R.

P l a i n

Gulf of Finland

St. Petersburg

Rybinsk Res.

Gorki Res.

Volga River

Kama R.

Sea

ESTONIA

L. Peipus

Volga River

Kuybyshev Res.

Riga

LATVIA

Moscow

Oka R.

Volga Upland

LITHUANIA

Western

Dvina R.

E u r o p e a n

Central

Russian

Upland

Oka-Don

Plain

Ural River

Neman R.

To Russia

BELARUS

Warsaw

Pripyat Marshes

Pripyat

Bug R.

Dnieper R.

Volgograd Res.

Volga River

KAZAKHSTAN

Caspian Depression

Ural River

A S I A

ND

Vistula R.

S t e p p e s

Aral Sea

Syr Darya

thian Mountains

Plain

Dniester R.

Kiev

Dnieper Lowland

Dnieper R.

Donets R.

Don R.

Don R.

Volga River

Volga R. Delta

Caspian

UKRAINE

UZBEKISTAN

Amu Darya

MOLDOVA

Mures R.

Prut R.

Sea Lowland

Odessa

Sea of Azov

Crimean Pen.

Caspian Sea

ROMANIA

Transylvanian Alps

Bucharest

Black R.

TURKMENISTAN

Danube River

BULGARIA

Balkan Mts.

Black Sea

Caucasus Mountains

Mt. Elbrus 18,510 ft.

GEORGIA

Baku

Balkan Peninsula

Bosporus

Istanbul

Sea of Marmara

AZERBAIJAN

ARMENIA

Mt. Olympus 9,570 ft.

Dardanelles

T U R K E Y

GREECE

Euboea

Lake Tuz

Lake Van

Lake Urmia

Tehran

Aegean Sea

Cyclades

Rhodes

Crete

Cyprus

LEBANON

SYRIA

IRAQ

I R A N

Sea

Political Map
Europe

Boundary Symbols

International boundary

Other boundary
(disputed or undefined)

☒ Small country

City Symbols

Barcelona ● ⎤ A city's relative size is
Glasgow ● ⎬ shown by the size of
Constanta ● ⎦ its symbol and lettering.

Moscow ⊛ National capital

Scale

0 100 200 300 400 miles

1 inch stands for 276 miles

Detailed legend on page 3

OCEAN

Hammerfest
Vardo
Barents Sea
Novaya Zemlya
Kolguyev I.
Murmansk
Kiruna
L. Inari
Oulu
Arkhangelsk
White Sea
Pechora R.
Onega R.
Ob R.
Northern Dvina R.

FINLAND
Vaasa
Syktyvkar
RUSSIA
Omsk

Tampere
L. Saimaa
Sukhona R.
Kamskoye Res.
Yekaterinburg

Turku
Helsinki
Lake Onega
Kirov
Vyatka
Perm
Chelyabinsk

Gulf of Finland
St. Petersburg
Lake Ladoga
Izhevsk
Ufa
70°E

Tallinn
ESTONIA
L. Peipus
Rybinsk Res.
Yaroslavl
Gorki Res.
Kazan
Kama R.
50°N

Riga
LATVIA
Tver
Volga R.
Nizhniy Novgorod
Oka R.
Kuybyshev Res.

LITHUANIA
Moscow
Samara
Orenburg

Vilnius
Western Dvina R.
Smolensk
Tula
Penza
Ural R.

Minsk
Neman R.
Saratov
Oral
KAZAKHSTAN
ASIA

BELARUS
Bryansk
Orel
Voronezh
Volgograd Res.
70°E

Bug R.
Pripyat R.
Kursk
Syr Darya

Chernobyl
Aral Sea

Lviv
Kiev
Kharkiv
Donets R.
Volgograd
Volga R.
UZBEKISTAN

UKRAINE
Dnieper R.
Donetsk
Don R.
Astrakhan
Amu Darya

Dniester R.
Dnipropetrovsk
Rostov-na-Donu
Volga R. Delta
40°N

MOLDOVA
Chisinau
Sea of Azov
TURKMENISTAN

Cluj-Napoca
Prut R.
Odessa
Kerch
Novorossiysk
Krasnodar
Groznyy
Caspian Sea
Ashgabat

ROMANIA
Sevastopol
Yalta
Black Sea

Bucharest
Danube R.
Constanta
Varna

Sofia
GEORGIA
Tbilisi
Baku
60°E

BULGARIA
Bosporus
ARMENIA
Yerevan
AZERBAIJAN

Plovdiv
Istanbul
Sea of Marmara
Lake Van
Lake Urmia

Thessaloniki
TURKEY
Ankara
Tehran

GREECE
Dardanelles
L. Tuz
IRAN

Euboea
Aegean Sea

Athens
30°N

Sea
Nicosia
SYRIA
IRAQ

Crete (Greece)
CYPRUS
LEBANON

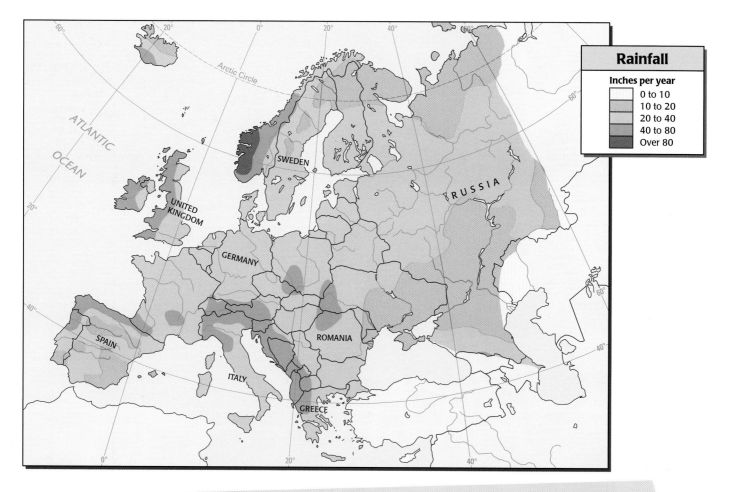

Rainfall

Inches per year
- 0 to 10
- 10 to 20
- 20 to 40
- 40 to 80
- Over 80

Focus on Highways of Water

- The Rhine and Danube Rivers and the rivers and canals that flow into them form a vast inland waterway.
- Barges and boats provide cheap transportation for raw materials and finished goods.
- The network's busiest river is the Rhine.

European Waterways

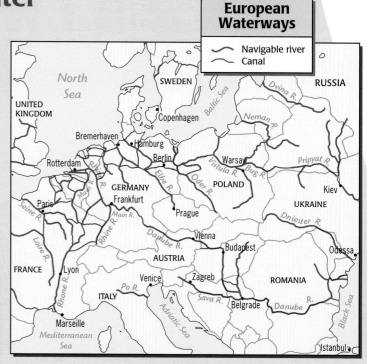

- Navigable river
- Canal

A river barge passes Frankfurt, Germany. The city sits on the banks of the busy Main River, which flows into the Rhine.

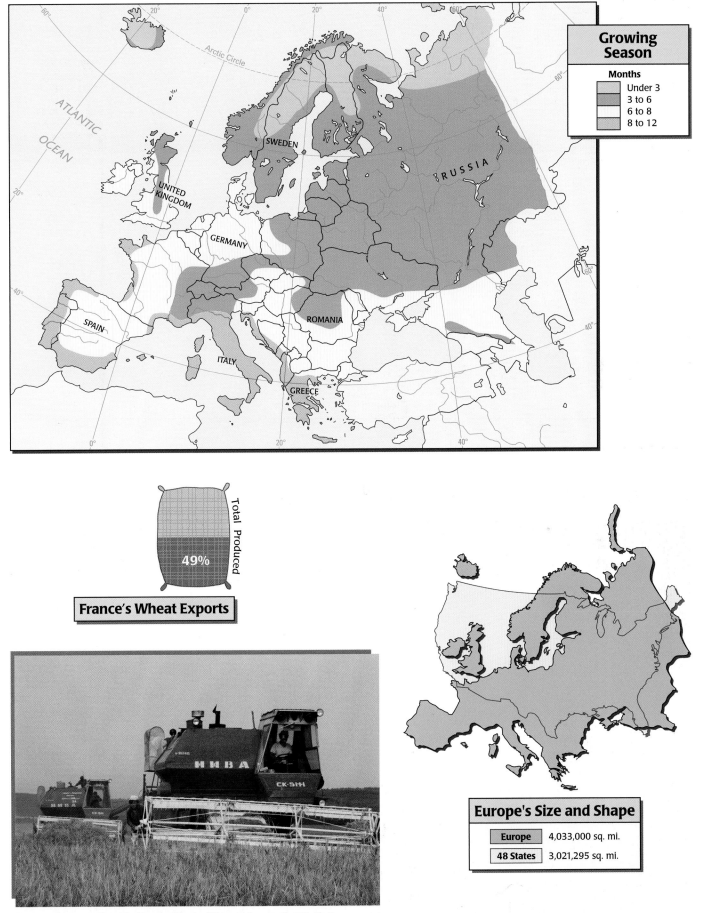

Growing Season

Months

	Under 3
	3 to 6
	6 to 8
	8 to 12

ATLANTIC OCEAN

SWEDEN

RUSSIA

UNITED KINGDOM

GERMANY

SPAIN

ROMANIA

ITALY

GREECE

Arctic Circle

France's Wheat Exports

Total Produced

49%

Europe's Size and Shape

Europe	4,033,000 sq. mi.
48 States	3,021,295 sq. mi.

Farmers harvest wheat in Russia. Most of Europe has a climate that favors farming.

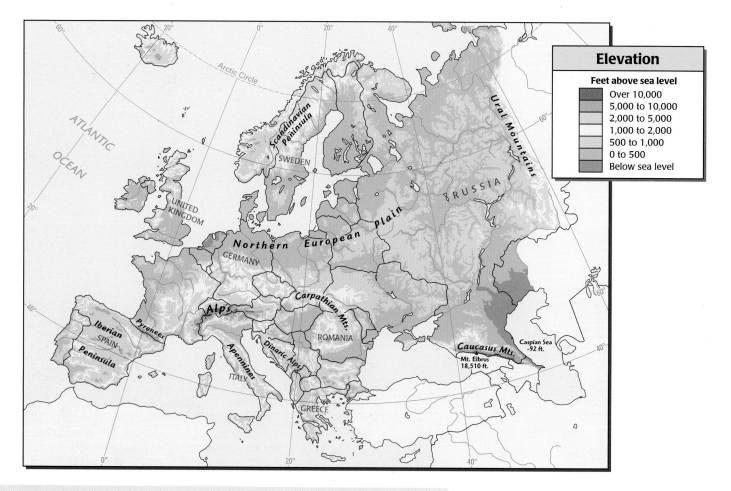

Elevation

Feet above sea level

- Over 10,000
- 5,000 to 10,000
- 2,000 to 5,000
- 1,000 to 2,000
- 500 to 1,000
- 0 to 500
- Below sea level

Focus on an Unnatural Landscape

- For centuries Europeans changed the landscape around them.
- European forests were cleared for farmland and to provide timber for ships and charcoal for industry.
- Early factories and growing cities polluted the air and water.

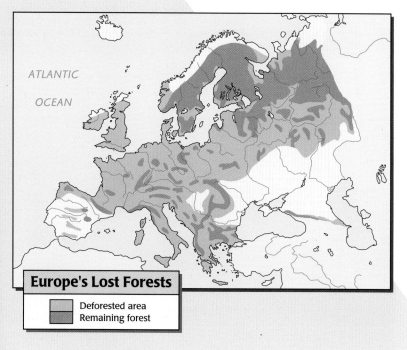

Europe's Lost Forests

- Deforested area
- Remaining forest

Industries began polluting Europe long ago. But recent laws have helped restore cleaner air and water.

Where Was *That* One Made?

Some of the best-known cars in the world are Mercedes-Benz, Fiat, Volkswagen, Rolls-Royce, Volvo, Ferrari, Jaguar, and Peugeot. Can you match these brands with the countries where they were first built?

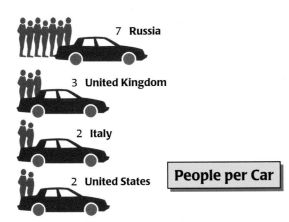

7 **Russia**

3 **United Kingdom**

2 **Italy**

2 **United States**

People per Car

Washing machines are assembled in a German factory. Germany is also the largest car manufacturer in Europe.

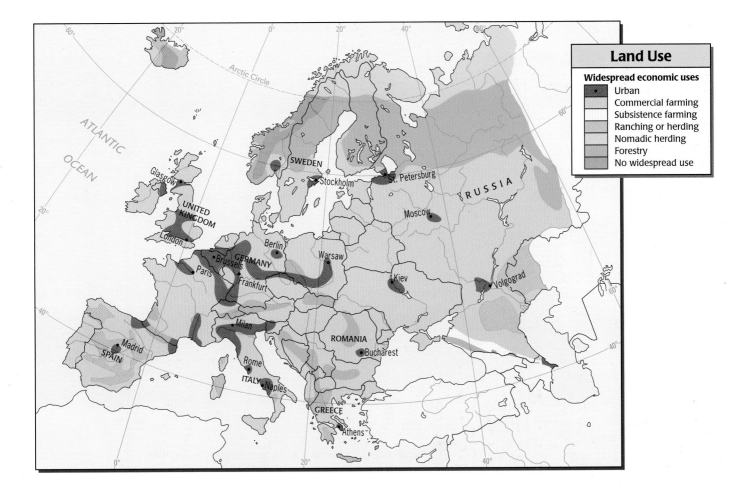

Land Use

Widespread economic uses

- Urban
- Commercial farming
- Subsistence farming
- Ranching or herding
- Nomadic herding
- Forestry
- No widespread use

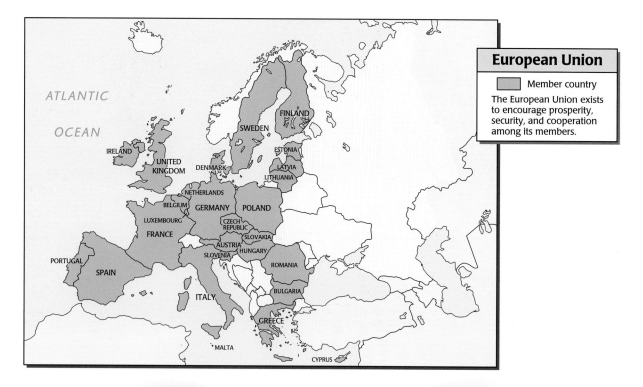

Parlez-vous Anglais?

English is the second-most widely spoken language in the world after Mandarin Chinese. About 400 million people use it daily. Another 300 million use it as their second language—often for business. French and Swedish executives may not speak each other's language, but both may speak English.

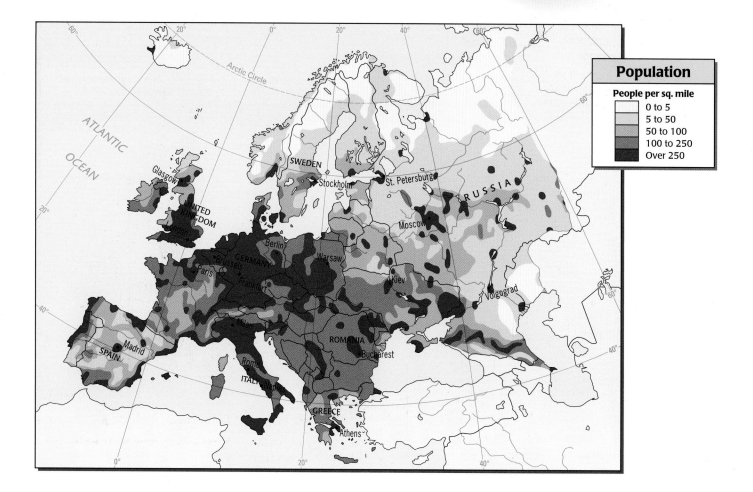

Rome's Colosseum was built almost 2,000 years ago, when Rome ruled the Mediterranean region and Western Europe. It is one of the world's most famous landmarks.

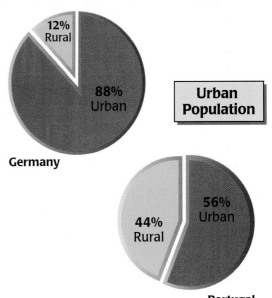

Urban Population

12% Rural

88% Urban

Germany

44% Rural

56% Urban

Portugal

Focus on the United Kingdom

- Great Britain and Ireland are the main islands of the British Isles.
- The country called the United Kingdom consists of Scotland, England, Wales (all on Great Britain), and Northern Ireland.
- The southern part of the island of Ireland is a separate country.

Families and friends relax at a park near the center of Edinburgh, the capital of Scotland.

100 mi.

Shetland Is. (U.K.)

Orkney Is.

ATLANTIC OCEAN

Hebrides

Loch Ness

Aberdeen

North Sea

SCOTLAND

Edinburgh

Glasgow

Great Britain

NORTHERN IRELAND

Belfast

Isle of Man (U.K.)

Leeds

Manchester

Liverpool

Irish Sea

Ireland

Shannon R.

Dublin

REPUBLIC OF IRELAND

Cork

WALES

Cardiff

ENGLAND

Birmingham

London

Bristol

Thames R.

Southampton

Strait of Dover

Celtic Sea

Isle of Wight

English Channel

FRANCE

Channel Islands (U.K.)

United Kingdom

⊛ London   National capital
★ Belfast   Secondary capital

Political Map
Russia and Its Neighbors

Boundary Symbols

○○○○○○○○	Continental boundary
‒ ‒ ‒ ‒ ‒	International boundary
▬▬▬▬▬	Former Soviet Union

City Symbols

Perm ●	
Vladivostok •	A city's relative size is shown by the size of its symbol and lettering.
Verkhoyansk •	

Moscow ⊛   National capital

Scale

0   250   500   750 miles

1 inch stands for 519 miles

Detailed legend on page 3

The Russian Orthodox Cathedral of St. Basil is located in the heart of Moscow, Russia's capital.

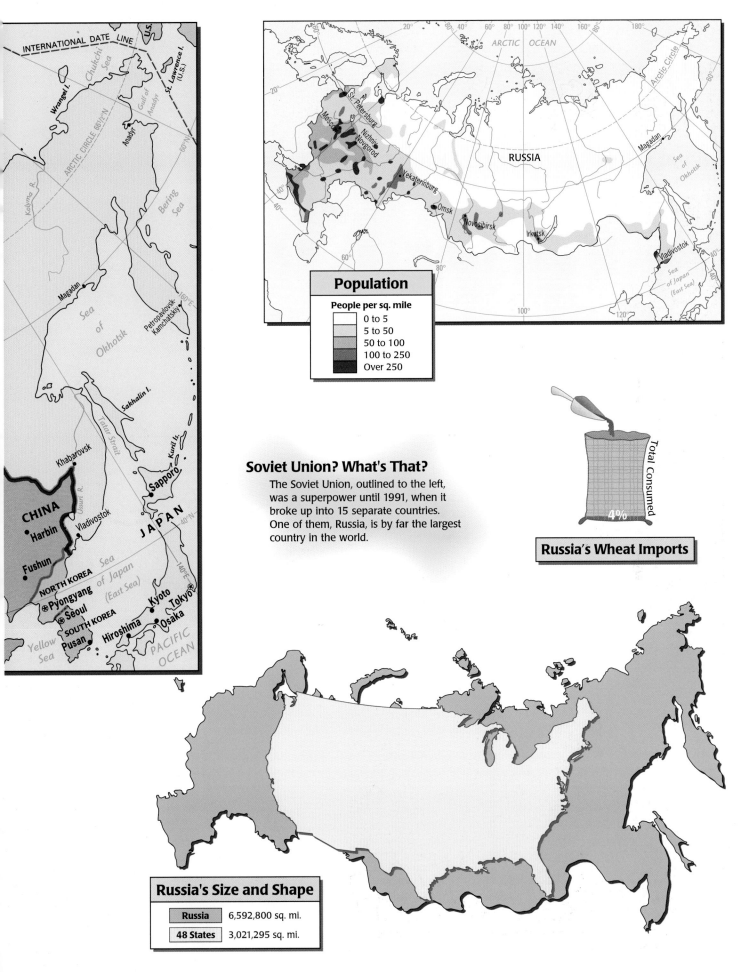

Population

People per sq. mile

- 0 to 5
- 5 to 50
- 50 to 100
- 100 to 250
- Over 250

Soviet Union? What's That?

The Soviet Union, outlined to the left, was a superpower until 1991, when it broke up into 15 separate countries. One of them, Russia, is by far the largest country in the world.

Total Consumed

4%

Russia's Wheat Imports

Russia's Size and Shape

Russia	6,592,800 sq. mi.
48 States	3,021,295 sq. mi.

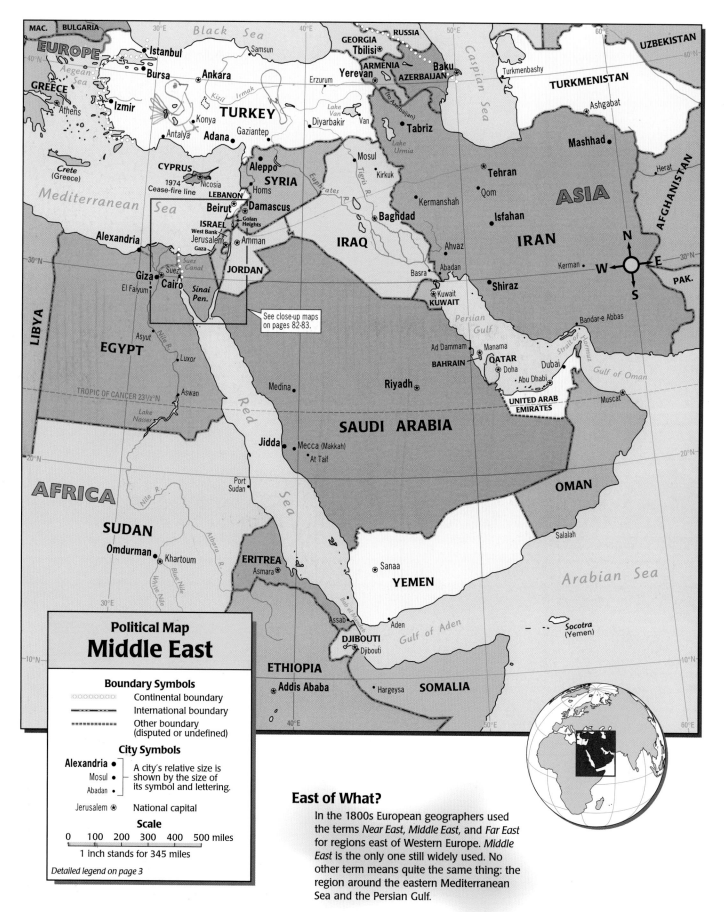

Political Map
Middle East

Boundary Symbols

○○○○○○○ Continental boundary

━━━━━━━ International boundary

- - - - - - - Other boundary
(disputed or undefined)

City Symbols

Alexandria ● | A city's relative size is
Mosul ● | shown by the size of
Abadan ● | its symbol and lettering.

Jerusalem ⊛ | National capital

Scale

| 0 | 100 | 200 | 300 | 400 | 500 miles |

1 inch stands for 345 miles

Detailed legend on page 3

East of What?

In the 1800s European geographers used the terms *Near East*, *Middle East*, and *Far East* for regions east of Western Europe. *Middle East* is the only one still widely used. No other term means quite the same thing: the region around the eastern Mediterranean Sea and the Persian Gulf.

Focus on Oil and OPEC

- Much of the world's oil is produced by OPEC—the Organization of Petroleum Exporting Countries.

- OPEC members Iran, Iraq, Kuwait, Qatar, Saudi Arabia, and the United Arab Emirates are all on the Persian Gulf.

- OPEC also includes Algeria, Libya, Nigeria, Angola, Ecuador, and Venezuela.

Pipelines carry oil many miles across the Saudi Arabian desert to ports on the Persian Gulf and the Red Sea.

| OPEC | Russia | U.S. | China | Mexico | Norway | Canada | U.K. | Others |

Leading Oil Producers

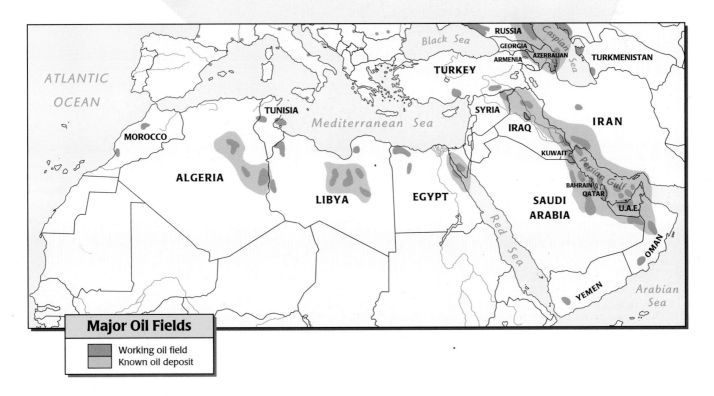

Major Oil Fields

- Working oil field
- Known oil deposit

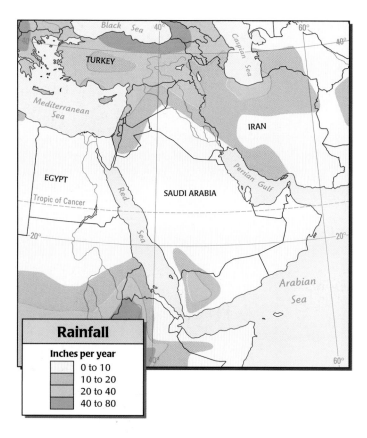

Rainfall

Inches per year

	0 to 10
	10 to 20
	20 to 40
	40 to 80

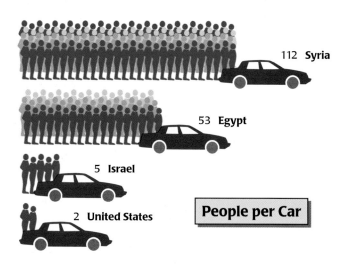

112	**Syria**
53	**Egypt**
5	**Israel**
2	**United States**

People per Car

How Can Salt Water Help?

Towing icebergs to the Middle East for fresh water is a tempting but very expensive idea. Instead, oil-rich countries here operate de-salting (*desalination*) plants that turn sea water into fresh water.

Focus on Israel's Changing Shape

- In 1967 Israel seized parts of Egypt, Jordan, and Syria during the Six Day War.
- Israel returned the Sinai Peninsula to Egypt in stages during 1975, 1979, and 1982.
- In 1994 Palestinians began administering the Gaza Strip and most of the West Bank.
- In 2005 Israel's government voted to remove Israeli settlements from Gaza Strip and the West Bank.

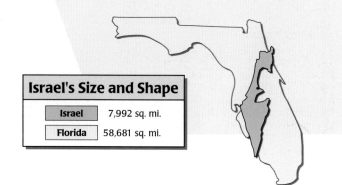

Israel's Size and Shape

Israel	7,992 sq. mi.
Florida	58,681 sq. mi.

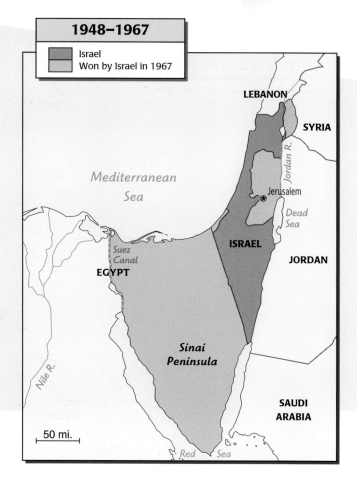

1948–1967

	Israel
	Won by Israel in 1967

50 mi.

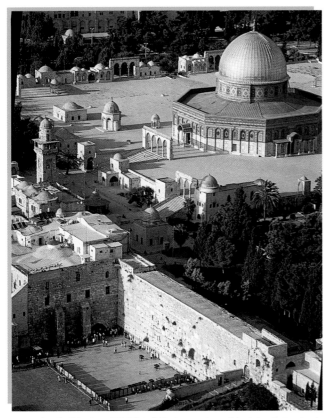

Jerusalem's Western Wall is all that remains of Judaism's ancient Temple. The nearby Dome of the Rock is the city's holiest Islamic shrine. Jerusalem is also a holy city for Christians.

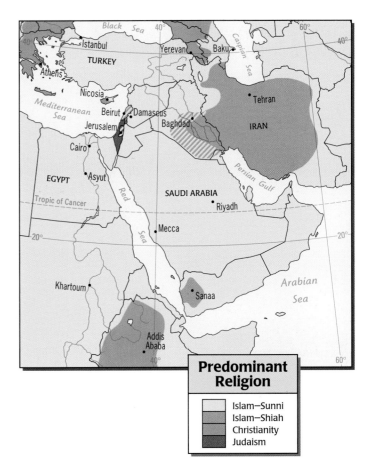

Predominant Religion

	Islam–Sunni
	Islam–Shiah
	Christianity
	Judaism

1975–1982

	Israel
	Adm. by Israel, claimed by others
	Returned to Egypt by Israel

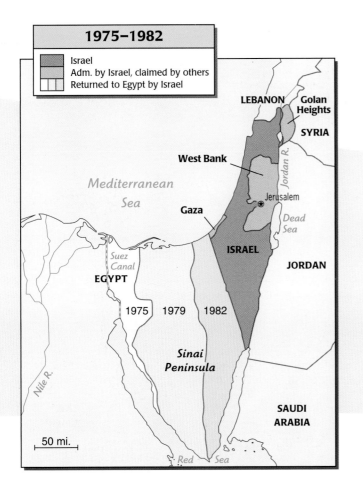

50 mi.

1994–Today

	Adm. by Israel, claimed by Syria
	Adm. by Palestinian Authority
	Adm. by Israel and by Palestinian Authority

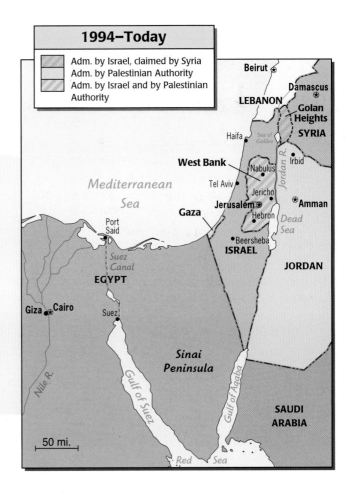

50 mi.

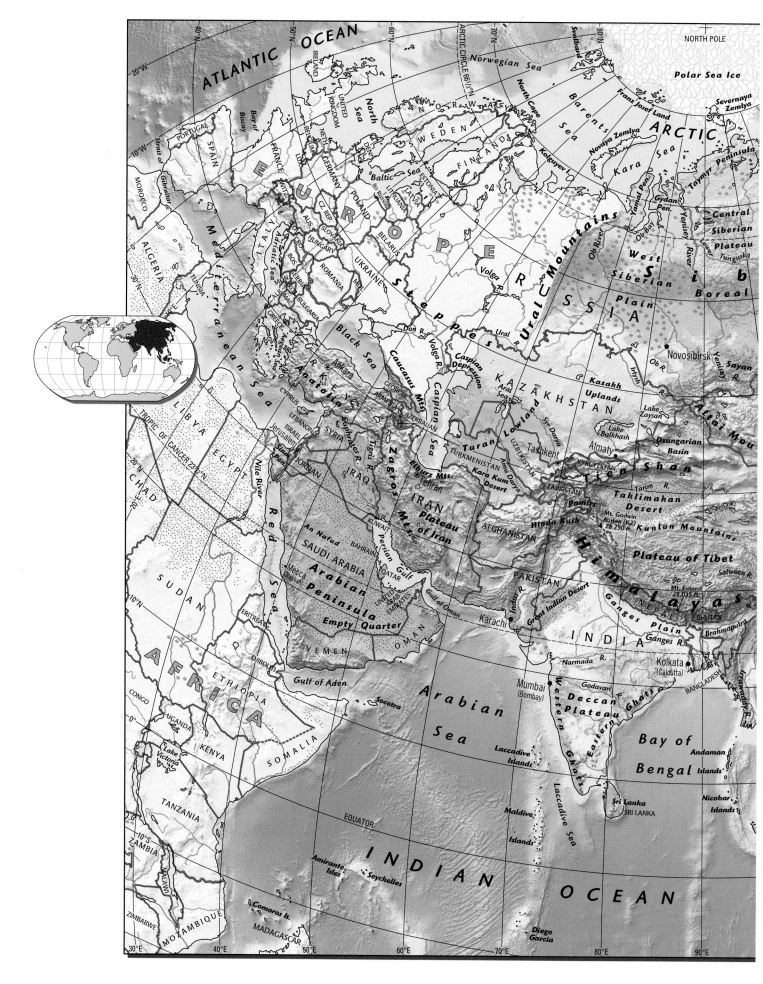

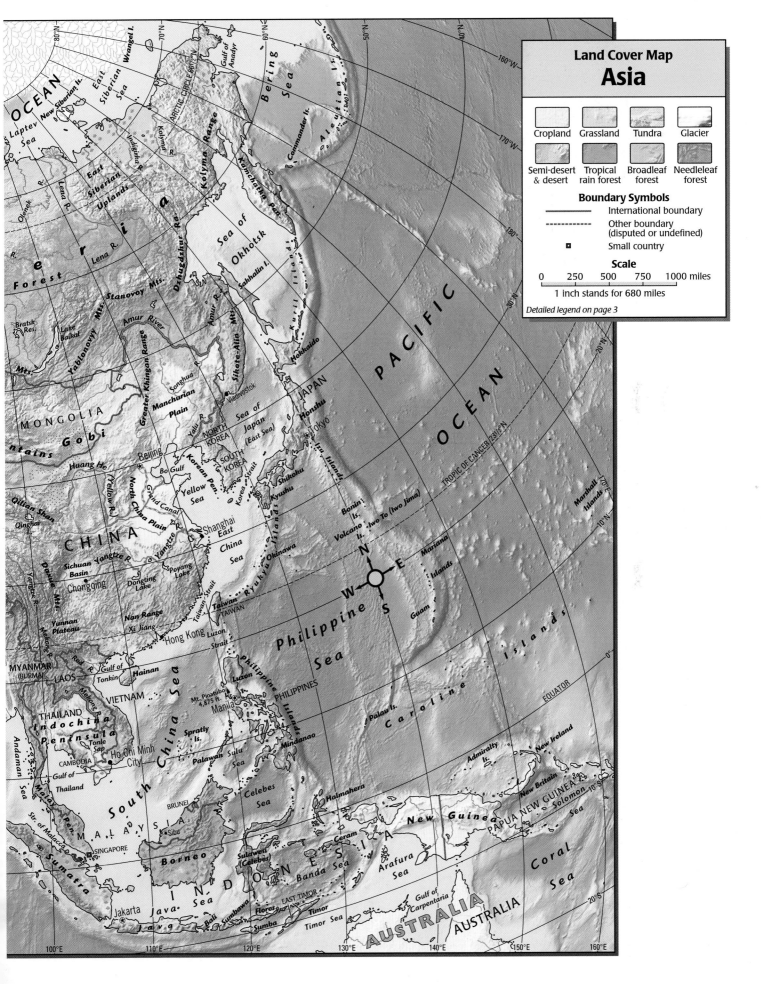

Land Cover Map
Asia

Cropland	Grassland	Tundra	Glacier
Semi-desert & desert	Tropical rain forest	Broadleaf forest	Needleleaf forest

Boundary Symbols
International boundary
Other boundary (disputed or undefined)
Small country

Scale
0   250   500   750   1000 miles
1 inch stands for 680 miles

Detailed legend on page 3

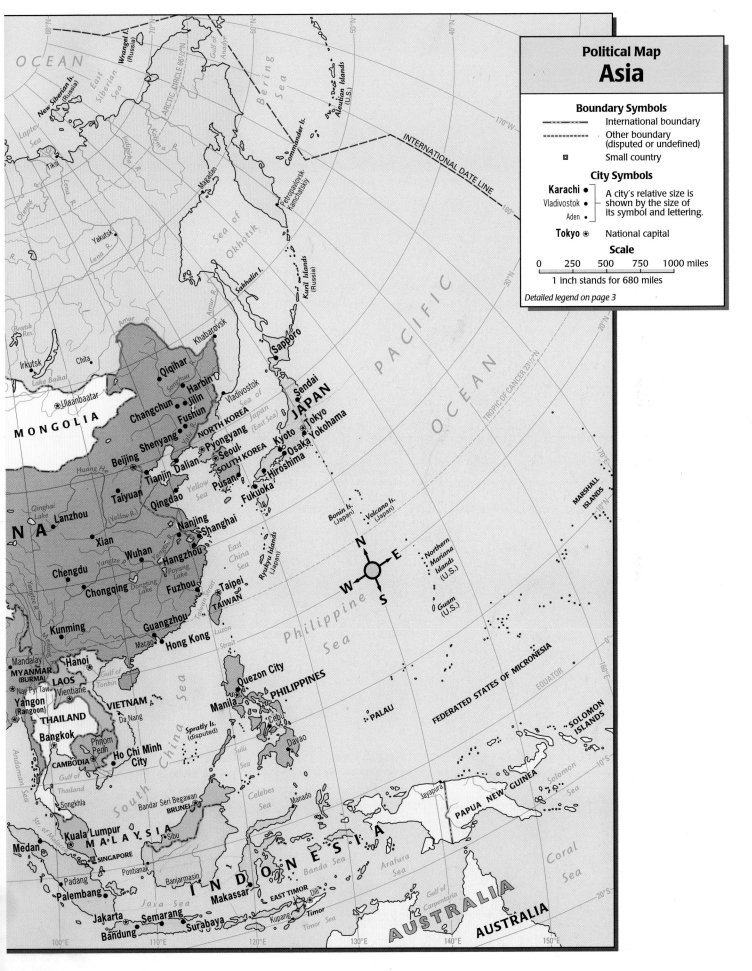

Political Map
Asia

Boundary Symbols

International boundary

Other boundary
(disputed or undefined)

⊡ Small country

City Symbols

Karachi •
Vladivostok •
Aden •

A city's relative size is
shown by the size of
its symbol and lettering.

Tokyo ⊛   National capital

Scale

0   250   500   750   1000 miles

1 inch stands for 680 miles

Detailed legend on page 3

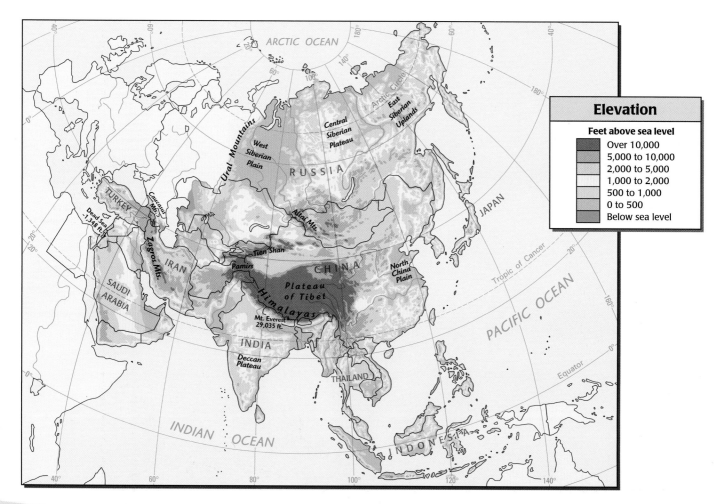

Elevation

Feet above sea level
- Over 10,000
- 5,000 to 10,000
- 2,000 to 5,000
- 1,000 to 2,000
- 500 to 1,000
- 0 to 500
- Below sea level

Focus on the Roof of the World

- The Himalayas are the world's highest mountain range.
- They form a massive barrier along northern Pakistan, India, Nepal, and Bhutan.
- To their north is China's high, dry Plateau of Tibet—the world's highest plateau.

A glacier flows down a valley in the Himalayas. In Sanskrit, the ancient language of India, *Himalaya* means "House of Snow."

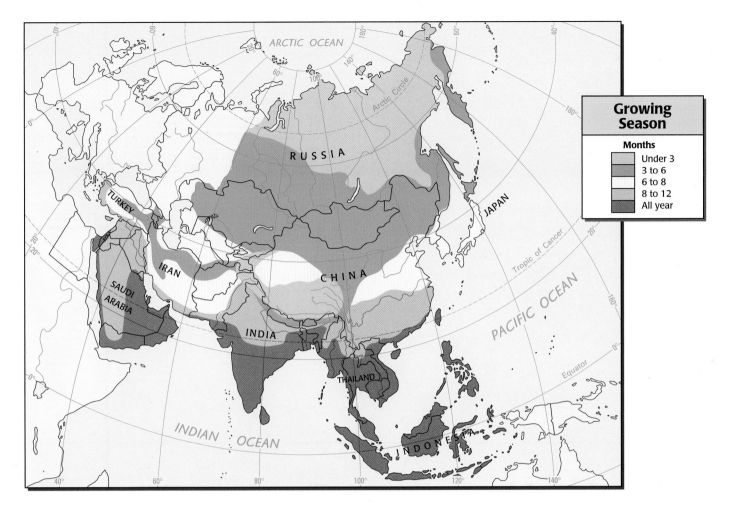

Growing Season

Months

- Under 3
- 3 to 6
- 6 to 8
- 8 to 12
- All year

Buddhist monks get ready to perform traditional music in Kathmandu, Nepal.

Elevation Cross Section

Feet above sea level

- Over 10,000
- 5,000 to 10,000
- 2,000 to 5,000
- 1,000 to 2,000
- 500 to 1,000
- 0 to 500

Area Shown

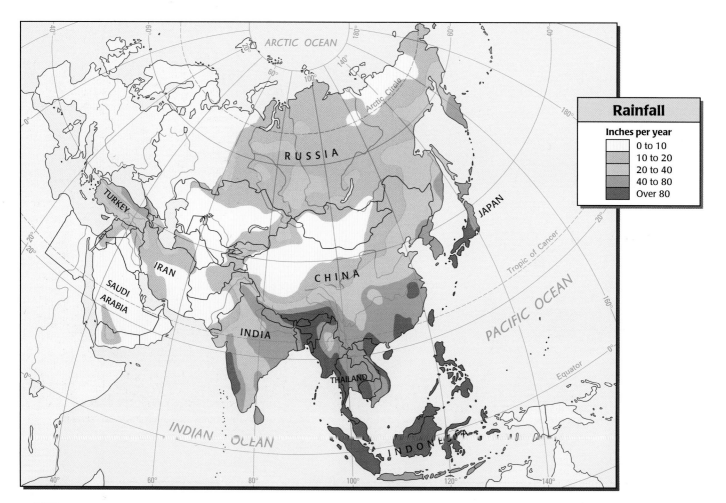

Rainfall

Inches per year

- 0 to 10
- 10 to 20
- 20 to 40
- 40 to 80
- Over 80

Focus on Monsoons

- Seasonal winds called *monsoons* control southern Asia's climate.
- Dry winter winds blow from central Asia toward the sea, keeping rain clouds away.
- In summer, the winds reverse. Wet ocean air rushes inland and brings torrents of rain.

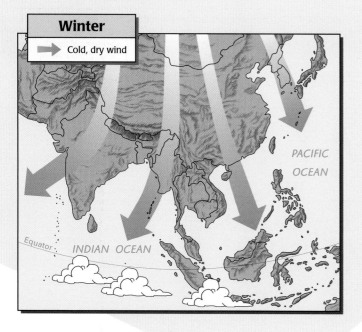

Winter

➡ Cold, dry wind

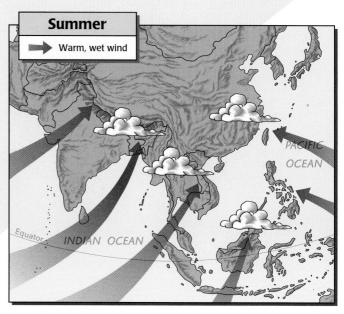

Summer

➡ Warm, wet wind

Japan's Size and Shape

Japan	145,883 sq. mi.
48 States	3,021,295 sq. mi.

Japan's Wheat Imports

95% Total Consumed

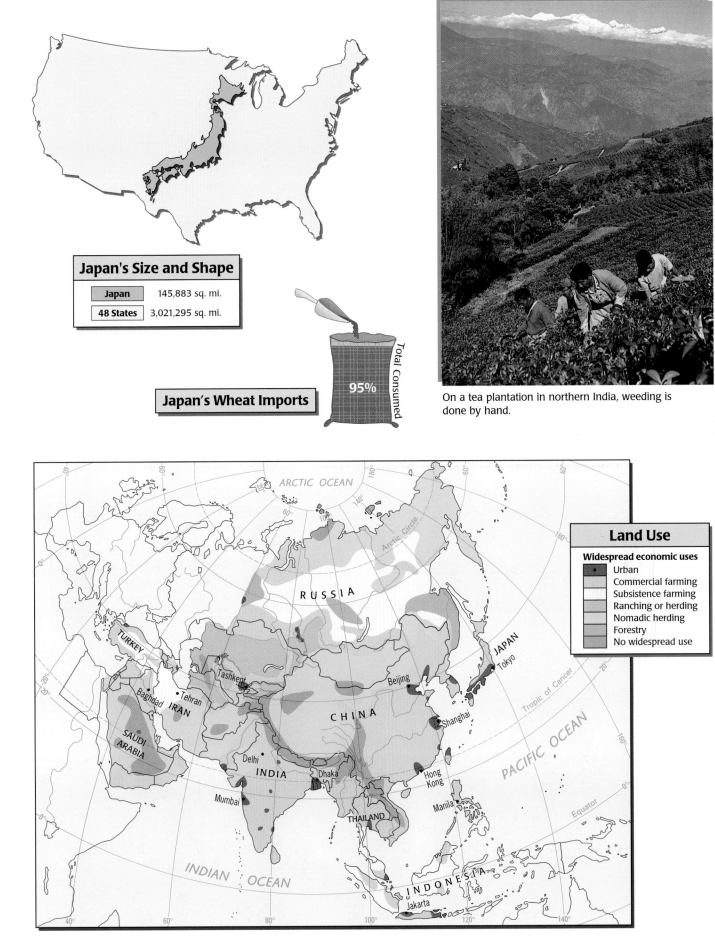

On a tea plantation in northern India, weeding is done by hand.

Land Use

Widespread economic uses
- Urban
- Commercial farming
- Subsistence farming
- Ranching or herding
- Nomadic herding
- Forestry
- No widespread use

ARCTIC OCEAN

Arctic Circle

RUSSIA

TURKEY

Tashkent

Baghdad • Tehran

IRAN

SAUDI ARABIA

Beijing

CHINA

JAPAN

Tokyo

Shanghai

Tropic of Cancer

PACIFIC OCEAN

Delhi •

INDIA

Dhaka

Hong Kong

Mumbai

Manila

THAILAND

INDIAN OCEAN

INDONESIA

Equator

Jakarta

Focus on Crowded Countries

- Southern and eastern Asia are among the world's most crowded regions.
- Six Asian countries have nearly half the world's population. Yet they occupy less than 11% of the world's land.
- Although Asia has many giant cities, most of its people still live in rural areas.

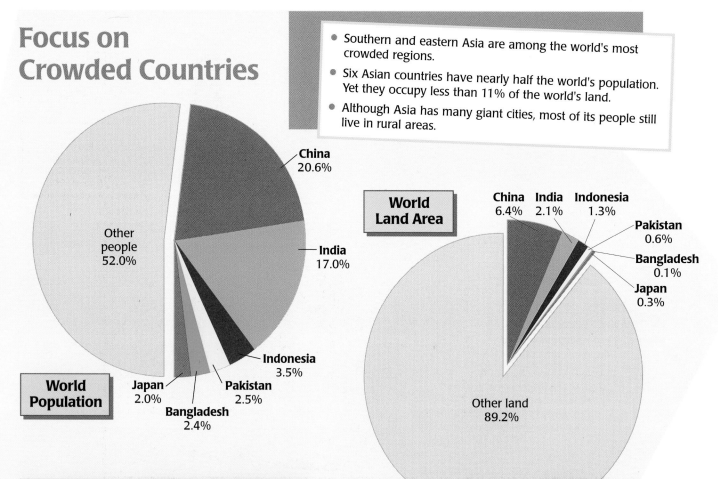

World Population

- China 20.6%
- India 17.0%
- Indonesia 3.5%
- Pakistan 2.5%
- Bangladesh 2.4%
- Japan 2.0%
- Other people 52.0%

World Land Area

- China 6.4%
- India 2.1%
- Indonesia 1.3%
- Pakistan 0.6%
- Bangladesh 0.1%
- Japan 0.3%
- Other land 89.2%

Throngs of people shop along Nanjing Road in Shanghai. About 17 million people live here, the largest of eastern China's many immense cities.

More than 70% of India's population lives away from urban areas. In western India, camels are bought and sold at rural fairs.

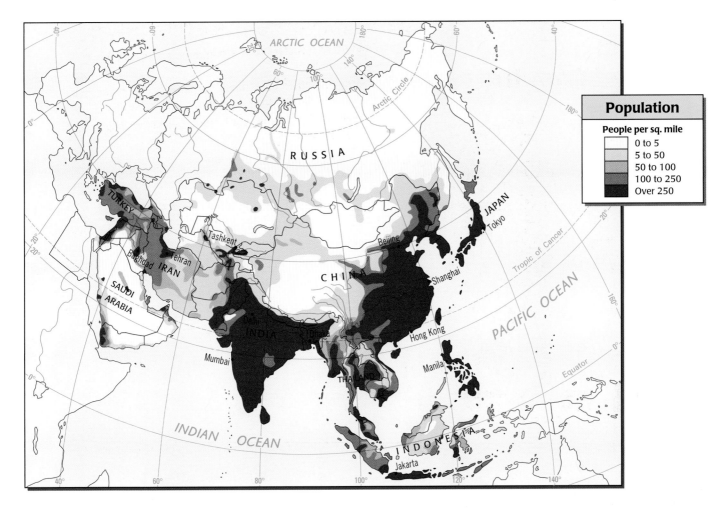

Population

People per sq. mile

- 0 to 5
- 5 to 50
- 50 to 100
- 100 to 250
- Over 250

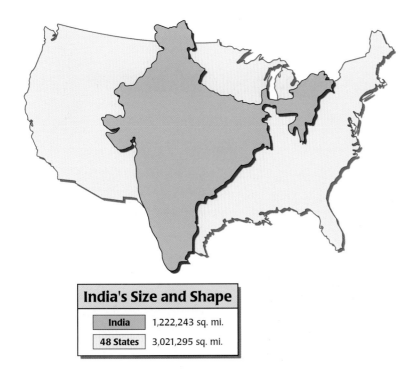

India's Size and Shape

India	1,222,243 sq. mi.
48 States	3,021,295 sq. mi.

Where Can You Find a Billion?

India has the second-largest population in the world, after China. With about one billion citizens, India has 3½ times as many people as the United States.

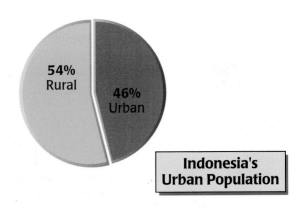

54% Rural

46% Urban

Indonesia's Urban Population

Focus on a Giant of Trade

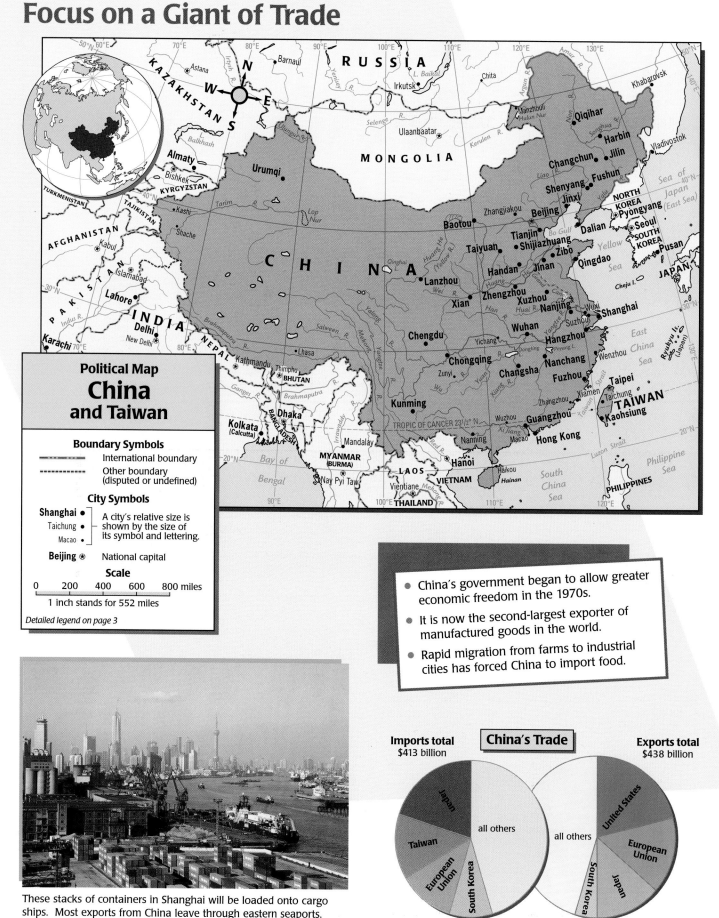

Political Map
China and Taiwan

Boundary Symbols

——————— International boundary

------------- Other boundary
(disputed or undefined)

City Symbols

Shanghai ●
Taichung ●
Macao ●
A city's relative size is shown by the size of its symbol and lettering.

Beijing ⊛ National capital

Scale

0   200   400   600   800 miles

1 inch stands for 552 miles

Detailed legend on page 3

- China's government began to allow greater economic freedom in the 1970s.
- It is now the second-largest exporter of manufactured goods in the world.
- Rapid migration from farms to industrial cities has forced China to import food.

These stacks of containers in Shanghai will be loaded onto cargo ships. Most exports from China leave through eastern seaports.

China's Trade

Imports total
$413 billion

Japan
Taiwan
European Union
South Korea
all others

Exports total
$438 billion

United States
European Union
Japan
South Korea
all others

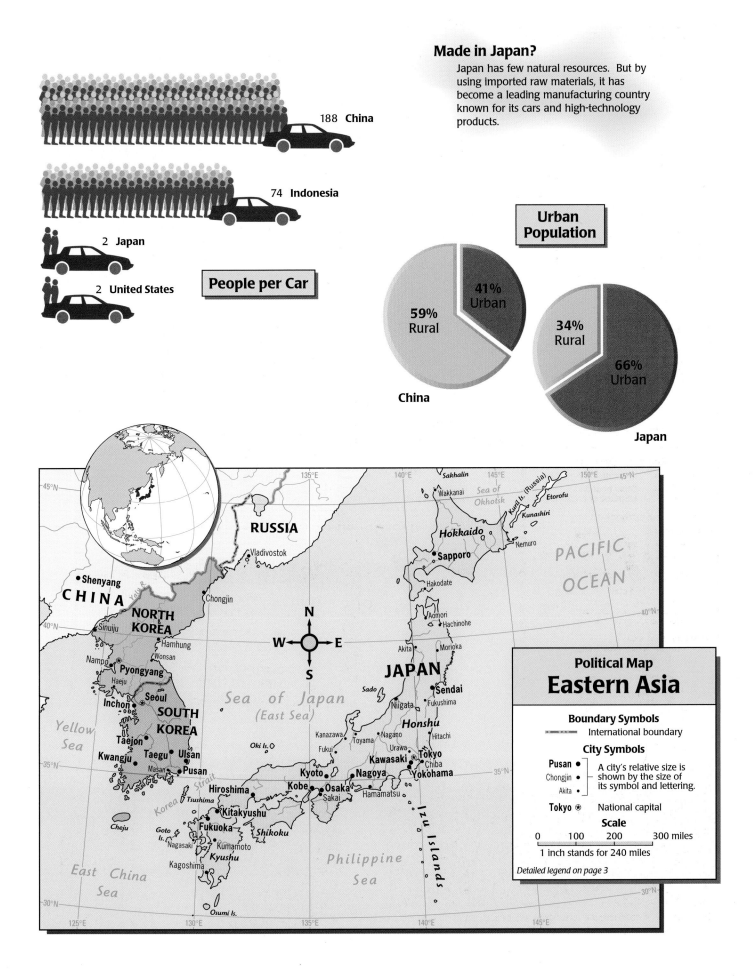

People per Car

188 China

74 Indonesia

2 Japan

2 United States

Made in Japan?

Japan has few natural resources. But by using imported raw materials, it has become a leading manufacturing country known for its cars and high-technology products.

Urban Population

59% Rural — 41% Urban
China

34% Rural — 66% Urban
Japan

Political Map
Eastern Asia

Boundary Symbols
International boundary

City Symbols

Pusan ●	A city's relative size is shown by the size of its symbol and lettering.
Chongjin ●	
Akita ●	

Tokyo ⊛ — National capital

Scale
0   100   200   300 miles
1 inch stands for 240 miles

Detailed legend on page 3

RUSSIA
Sakhalin
Wakkanai
Sea of Okhotsk
Kuril Is. (Russia)
Etorofu
Kunashiri
Nemuro
Hokkaido
Sapporo
PACIFIC OCEAN
Hakodate
Vladivostok
Shenyang
Chongjin
CHINA
NORTH KOREA
Sinuiju
Hamhung
Wonsan
Nampo
Pyongyang
Haeju
Inchon
Seoul
SOUTH KOREA
Taejon
Kwangju
Taegu
Ulsan
Masan
Pusan
Yellow Sea
Cheju
Goto Is.
Tsushima
Korea Strait
Hiroshima
Kitakyushu
Fukuoka
Nagasaki
Kumamoto
Kagoshima
Kyushu
Shikoku
East China Sea
Osumi Is.
Aomori
Hachinohe
Akita
Morioka
JAPAN
Sado
Sendai
Niigata
Fukushima
Honshu
Kanazawa
Toyama
Nagano
Hitachi
Fukui
Urawa
Kawasaki
Tokyo
Chiba
Kyoto
Nagoya
Yokohama
Kobe
Osaka
Sakai
Hamamatsu
Izu Islands
Philippine Sea
Sea of Japan (East Sea)
Oki Is.

N W E S

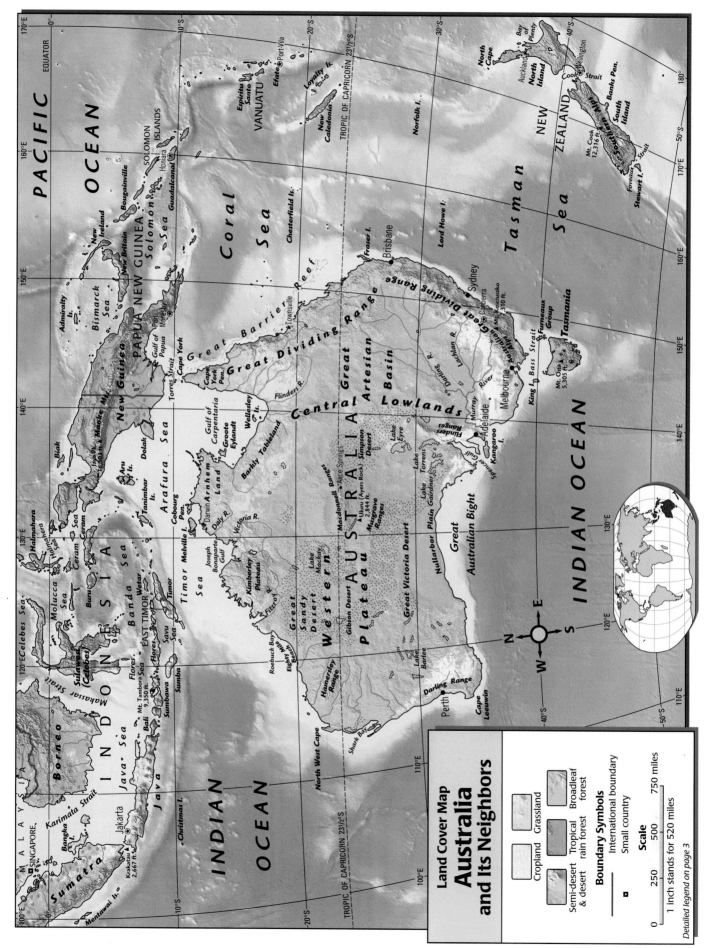

PACIFIC OCEAN

EQUATOR

Bougainville

New Ireland

New Britain

Admiralty Is.

Bismarck Sea

SOLOMON ISLANDS

Solomon Sea

Guadalcanal

Honiara

Coral Sea

Chesterfield Is.

Espiritu Santo

VANUATU

Efate Port-Vila

New Caledonia

Loyalty Is.

TROPIC OF CAPRICORN 23½°S

Norfolk I.

Lord Howe I.

Bay of Plenty

North Cape

Auckland North Island

Cook Strait

Banks Pen.

Wellington

NEW ZEALAND

South Island

Mt. Cook 12,316 ft.

Foveaux Strait

Stewart I.

Tasman Sea

Tasmania

Furneaux Group

King I. Bass Strait

Mt. Ossa 5,305 ft.

Melbourne

Australian Alps

Mt. Kosciuszko 7,310 ft.

Canberra

Sydney

Great Dividing Range

Brisbane

Fraser I.

Great Barrier Reef

Townsville

Cape York

Torres Strait

Cape York Pen.

Great Dividing Range

Great Artesian Basin

Central Lowlands

Darling R.

Lachlan R.

Murrumbidgee R.

Murray River

Adelaide

Flinders Ranges

Kangaroo I.

Spencer Gulf

Lake Eyre

Lake Torrens

Lake Gairdner

Great Australian Bight

Nullarbor Plain

Great Victoria Desert

AUSTRALIA

Great Western Plateau

Uluru (Ayers Rock) 2,844 ft.

Alice Springs

Macdonnell Ranges

Simpson Desert

Musgrave Ranges

Lake Amadeus

Lake Mackay

Great Sandy Desert

Gibson Desert

Tanami Desert

Barkly Tableland

Groote Eylandt

Gulf of Carpentaria

Wellesley Is.

Flinders R.

Arnhem Land

Darwin

Daly R.

Victoria R.

Joseph Bonaparte Gulf

Kimberley Plateau

Fitzroy R.

Roebuck Bay

Eighty Mile Beach

North West Cape

Hamersley Range

Lake Disappointment

Lake Carnegie

Lake Barlee

Darling Range

Shark Bay

Perth

Cape Leeuwin

INDIAN OCEAN

Melville I.

Cobourg Pen.

Arafura Sea

Timor Sea

Timor

EAST TIMOR

Wetar

Sumba

Savu Sea

Flores Sea

Flores

Sumbawa

Bali

Mt. Tambora 9,350 ft.

Lombok

Java Sea

Java

Jakarta

Madura

INDONESIA

Banda Sea

Buru

Ceram

Ceram Sea

Molucca Sea

Halmahera

Celebes Sea

Sulawesi (Celebes)

Makassar Strait

Borneo

MALAYSIA

SINGAPORE

Bangka I.

Karimata Strait

Sumatra

Krakatau 2,667 ft.

Christmas I.

Mentawai Is.

INDIAN OCEAN

TROPIC OF CAPRICORN 23½°S

Aru Is.

Tanimbar Is.

Dolak

Biak

Mt. Maoke 16,503 ft.

New Guinea

PAPUA NEW GUINEA

Gulf of Papua

Port Moresby

Haruku Sea

PACIFIC

OCEAN

N E W

Z E A L A N D

Tasman Sea

Australian Alps

INDIAN OCEAN

N
W — E
S

Land Cover Map
Australia
and Its Neighbors

Cropland	Grassland
Semi-desert & desert	Broadleaf forest
Tropical rain forest	

Boundary Symbols
International boundary
Small country

Scale
0   250   500   750 miles
1 inch stands for 520 miles

Detailed legend on page 3

Longitude markings: 100°E, 110°E, 120°E, 130°E, 140°E, 150°E, 160°E, 170°E, 180°
Latitude markings: EQUATOR, 10°S, 20°S, 30°S, 40°S, 50°S

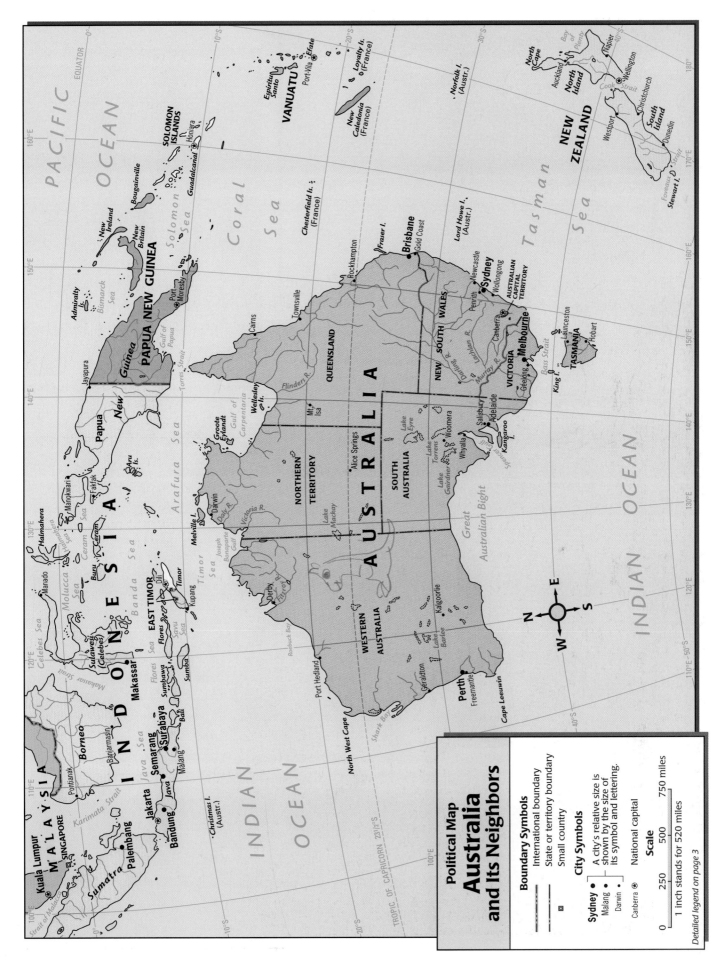

PACIFIC OCEAN

EQUATOR

VANUATU
Espiritu Santo
Port-Vila • Efate
Loyalty Is. (France)
New Caledonia (France)

SOLOMON ISLANDS
Bougainville
Honiara ✲
Guadalcanal

New Ireland
New Britain
Bismarck Sea
Admiralty Is.
Solomon Sea

PAPUA NEW GUINEA
Port Moresby
Gulf of Papua
New Guinea
Papua
Jayapura
Torres Strait

Chesterfield Is. (France)

Coral Sea

Fraser I.
Brisbane
Gold Coast

Lord Howe I. (Austr.)

Norfolk I. (Austr.)

North Cape
Bay of Plenty
Napier
Wellington
North Island
Auckland
Cook Strait
NEW ZEALAND
Christchurch
South Island
Westport
Dunedin
Foveaux Str.
Stewart I.

Tasman Sea

Rockhampton
Townsville
Cairns

QUEENSLAND

Mt. Isa

Wellesley Is.
Gulf of Carpentaria
Groote Eylandt
Flinder R.

NORTHERN TERRITORY

Alice Springs

AUSTRALIA

Newcastle
Sydney
Wollongong
Penrith
AUSTRALIAN CAPITAL TERRITORY
NEW SOUTH WALES
Canberra ✲
Darling R.
Lachlan R.
Murray R.
VICTORIA
Melbourne
Geelong
Launceston
TASMANIA
Hobart
King I.
Bass Strait

Lake Eyre
SOUTH AUSTRALIA
Lake Torrens
Lake Gairdner
Salisbury
Adelaide
Woomera
Whyalla
Kangaroo I.
Spencer G.

Lake Mackay

WESTERN AUSTRALIA

Lake Bardee

Kalgoorlie
Lake Carnegie

Great Australian Bight

INDIAN OCEAN

E
N — S
W

Geraldton
Perth
Freemantle
Cape Leeuwin

Shark Bay
North West Cape

Port Hedland
Roebuck Bay
Derby
Fitzroy R.

Darwin
Melville I.
Daly R.
Victoria R.
Joseph Bonaparte Gulf
Kupang
Timor
Dili
EAST TIMOR
Flores
Savu Sea
Timor Sea
Arafura Sea

INDIAN OCEAN

Sumba
Sumbawa
Bali
Java Sea
Flores Sea
Banda Sea
Makassar
Sulawesi (Celebes)
Celebes Sea
Ceram Sea
Ceram
Buru
Molucca Sea
Halmahera
Manado
Fakfak
Manokwari
Aru Is.

INDONESIA

Borneo
Banjarmasin
Pontianak
Makassar Strait

Malang
Surabaya
Semarang
Bandung
Jakarta
Java
Malang
Palembang
Sumatra
Karimata Strait

MALAYSIA
Kuala Lumpur
SINGAPORE
Strait of Malacca

Christmas I. (Austr.)

TROPIC OF CAPRICORN 23½°S

Political Map
Australia and Its Neighbors

Boundary Symbols
International boundary
State or territory boundary
Small country

City Symbols
Sydney ● A city's relative size is shown by the size of
Malang • its symbol and lettering.
Darwin •

Canberra ✲ National capital

Scale
0 250 500 750 miles
1 inch stands for 520 miles

Detailed legend on page 3

10°S
20°S
30°S
40°S
50°S

0°
100°E 110°E 120°E 130°E 140°E 150°E 160°E 170°E 180°

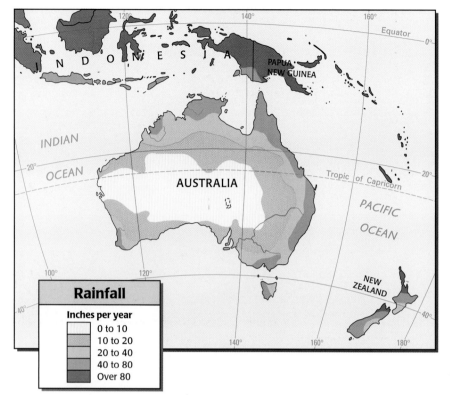

Rainfall

Inches per year

- 0 to 10
- 10 to 20
- 20 to 40
- 40 to 80
- Over 80

The rain forest of Papua New Guinea is hot and wet all year long.

Only three countries have more geysers than New Zealand. Dozens of geysers can be found on North Island.

You Mean It Gets *That* Cold?

Dry desert regions cool off quickly when the sun goes down. It is said that the Aborigines of the Australian desert talked of a "three-dog-night"—a night so cold you had to curl up with three dogs to stay warm.

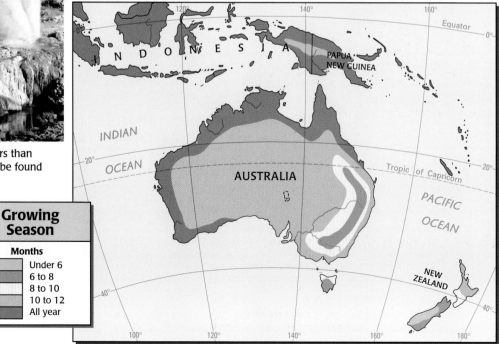

Growing Season

Months

- Under 6
- 6 to 8
- 8 to 10
- 10 to 12
- All year

Focus on Australia's Isolation

- Sea level dropped during the Ice Ages, exposing land between most continents. Animals crossed from continent to continent on the exposed land.

- But Asian species never reached Australia. Deep seas east of Borneo remained a watery barrier.

- As a result, many Australian animals and plants developed in unique ways.

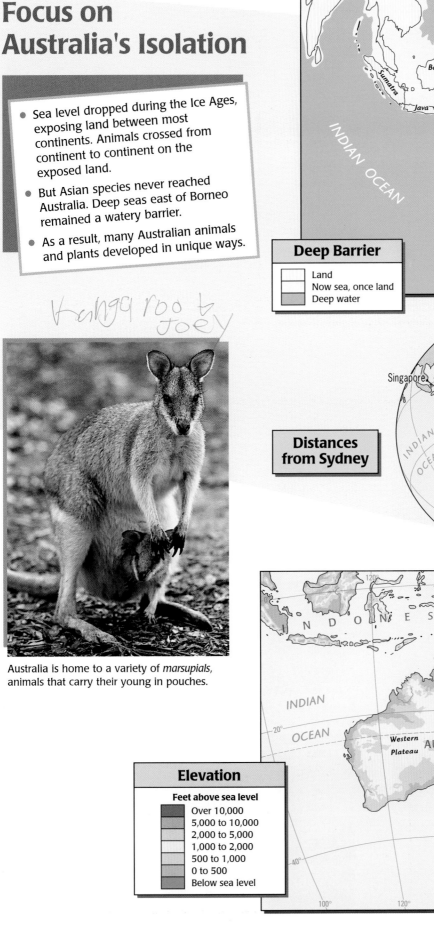

Australia is home to a variety of *marsupials*, animals that carry their young in pouches.

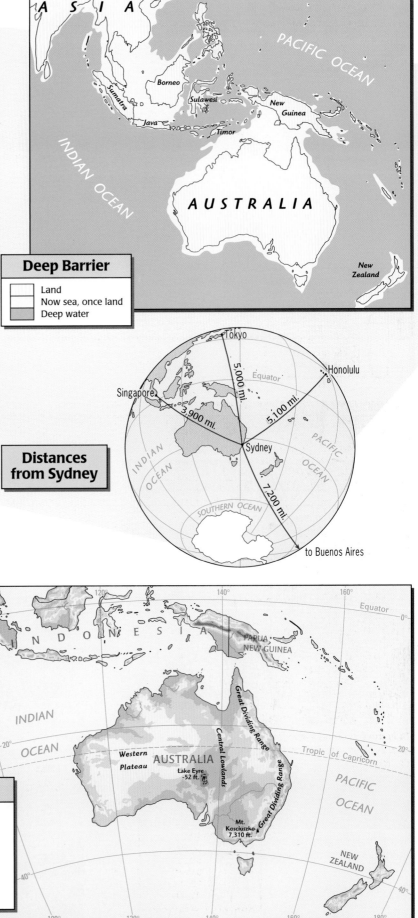

Deep Barrier

	Land
	Now sea, once land
	Deep water

Distances from Sydney

Tokyo
5,000 mi.
Honolulu
5,100 mi.
Singapore
3,900 mi.
Sydney
7,200 mi.
to Buenos Aires

Elevation

Feet above sea level

	Over 10,000
	5,000 to 10,000
	2,000 to 5,000
	1,000 to 2,000
	500 to 1,000
	0 to 500
	Below sea level

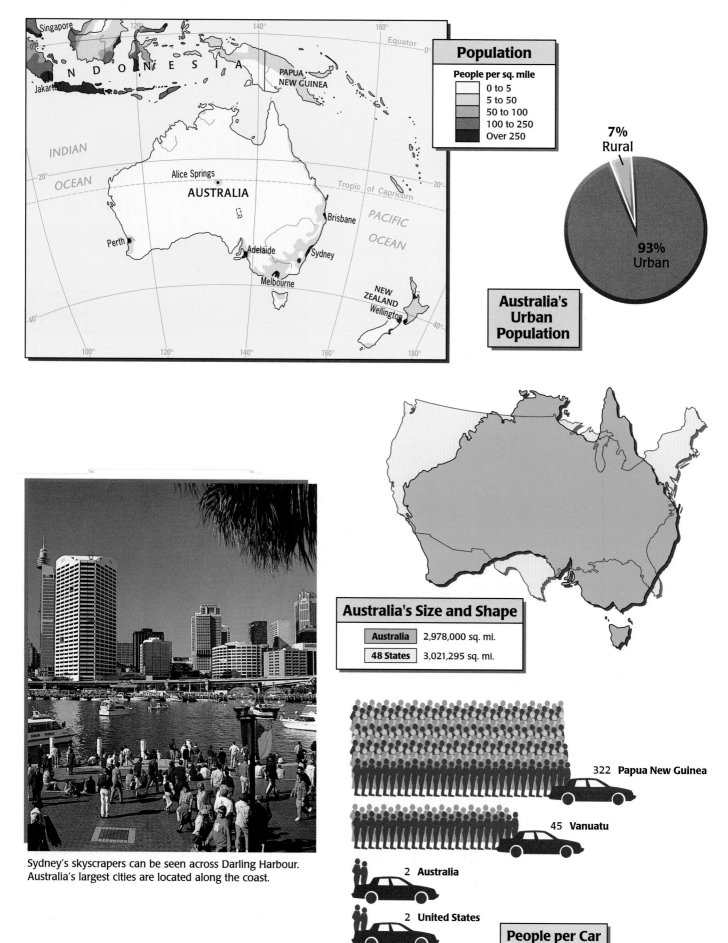

Population

People per sq. mile
- 0 to 5
- 5 to 50
- 50 to 100
- 100 to 250
- Over 250

7% Rural

93% Urban

Australia's Urban Population

Sydney's skyscrapers can be seen across Darling Harbour. Australia's largest cities are located along the coast.

Australia's Size and Shape

| Australia | 2,978,000 sq. mi. |
| 48 States | 3,021,295 sq. mi. |

322 **Papua New Guinea**

45 **Vanuatu**

2 **Australia**

2 **United States**

People per Car

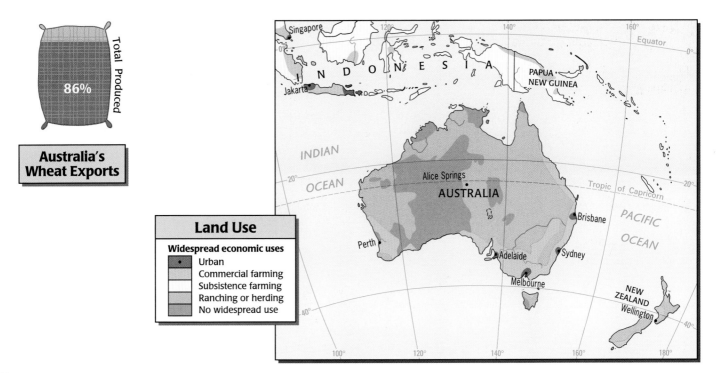

Total Produced

86%

Australia's Wheat Exports

Land Use

Widespread economic uses
- Urban
- Commercial farming
- Subsistence farming
- Ranching or herding
- No widespread use

Focus on People of the Pacific

- People first settled the Pacific islands about 60,000 years ago.
- In simple boats, they sailed from island to island across the ocean.
- They probably came from Asia. But one theory is that Easter Island was reached from South America.

The traditional canoes of Micronesia are made from painstakingly hollowed-out logs.

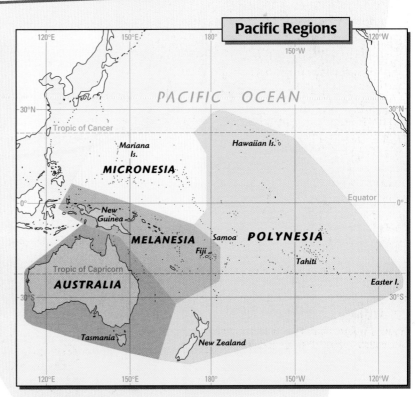

Pacific Regions

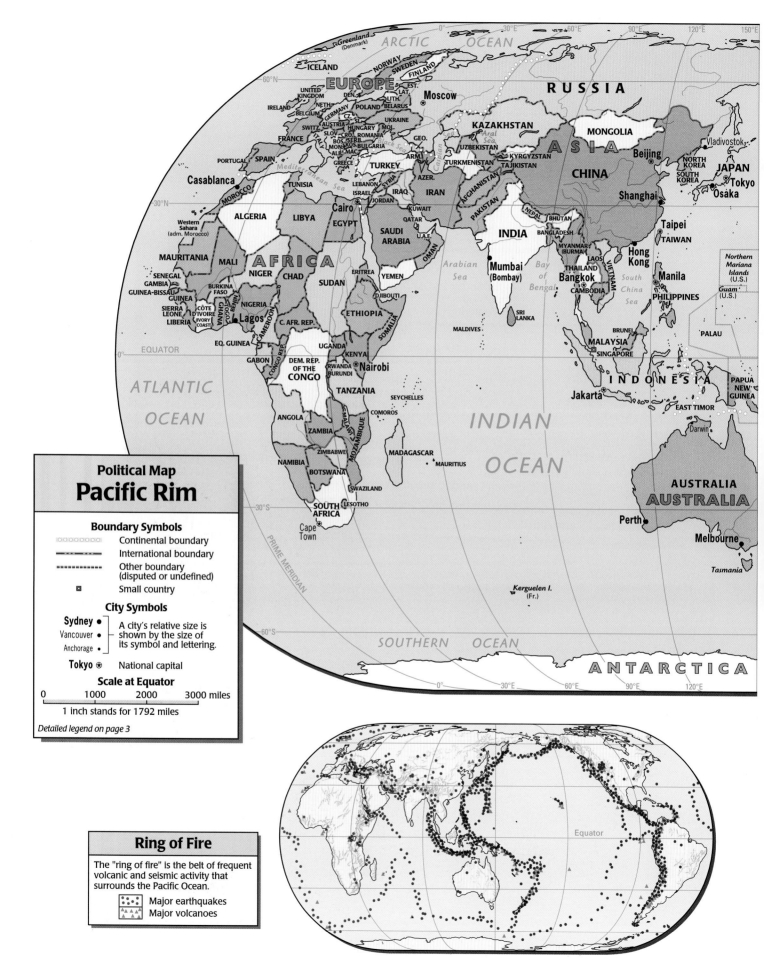

Political Map
Pacific Rim

Boundary Symbols
- Continental boundary
- International boundary
- Other boundary (disputed or undefined)
- Small country

City Symbols

Sydney • — A city's relative size is shown by the size of its symbol and lettering.

Vancouver •

Anchorage •

Tokyo ⊛ National capital

Scale at Equator

0 — 1000 — 2000 — 3000 miles

1 inch stands for 1792 miles

Detailed legend on page 3

Ring of Fire

The "ring of fire" is the belt of frequent volcanic and seismic activity that surrounds the Pacific Ocean.

- Major earthquakes
- Major volcanoes

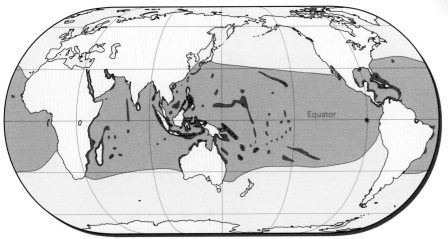

These Rocks Are *Alive?*

Coral is the rock-like substance formed by the outer skeletons of tiny sea animals. Their skeletons fuse as new coral colonies grow on top of old ones. In time, enough coral builds up to form a reef or an island.

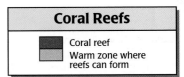

Coral Reefs	
■	Coral reef
■	Warm zone where reefs can form

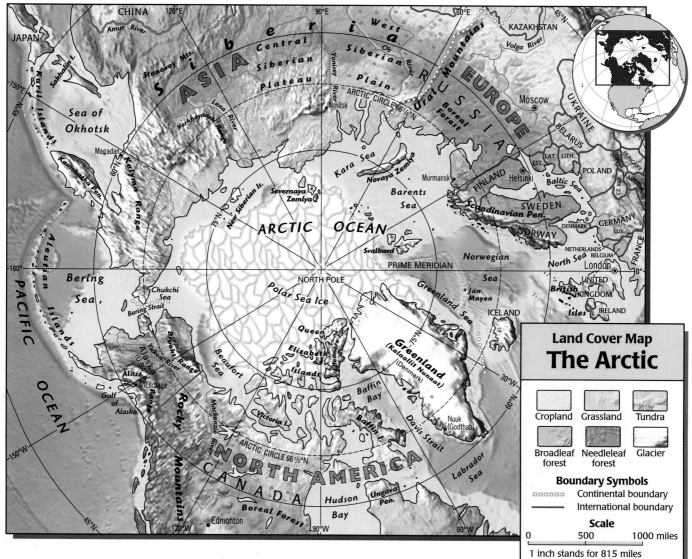

Land Cover Map
The Arctic

Cropland	Grassland	Tundra
Broadleaf forest	Needleleaf forest	Glacier

Boundary Symbols

ooooooo Continental boundary

—————— International boundary

Scale

0   500   1000 miles

1 inch stands for 815 miles

Detailed legend on page 3

Focus on the Frozen North

- Land that is frozen much or all of the year is called *permafrost*.
- Seasonal permafrost becomes deep mud in summer, threatening roads and buildings.

Traditional fur clothing helps protect hunters in northern Canada from the dangerous Arctic cold.

Permafrost

■	Continuous permafrost
■	Scattered permafrost

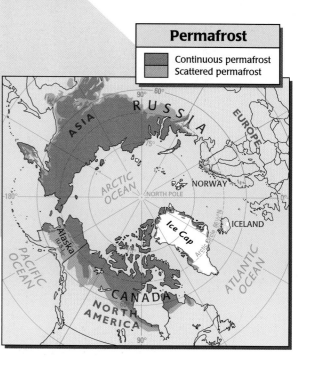

Focus on the Cold Continent

- Ice and snow cover 98% of Antarctica.
- Away from the coast, it is too cold and dry for most living things.
- Antarctica's ice cap holds 70% of the world's fresh-water supply.

Penguins are numerous along Antarctica's coast. Only insects live in the harsh interior.

Size and Shape

Antarctica	5,400,000 sq. mi.
48 States	3,021,295 sq. mi.

Cross Section

The ice cap on the Polar Plateau is up to 2½ miles thick.

SOUTHERN OCEAN
Weddell Sea
Queen Maud Land
SOUTH POLE
Antarctic Peninsula
Polar Plateau
Ice Cap
Ice Cap
SOUTHERN OCEAN
90°W
90°E

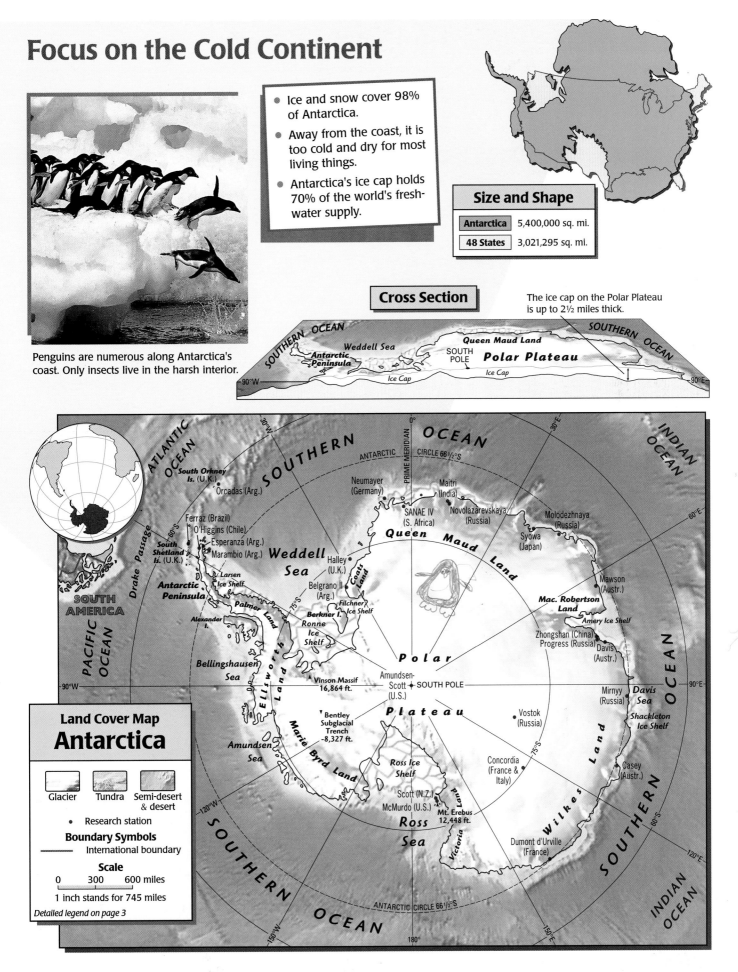

Land Cover Map
Antarctica

Glacier | Tundra | Semi-desert & desert

- Research station

Boundary Symbols
— International boundary

Scale
0   300   600 miles

1 inch stands for 745 miles

Detailed legend on page 3

MAP PROJECTIONS

Map projections are the means by which the curved surface of the earth is transferred to the flat surface of a map. There are an infinite number of map projections, but none is as accurate as a globe. Because the earth is a sphere, a globe is its only perfect model. A globe simultaneously shows accurate shapes, sizes, distances, and directions. No world map shows all four of these properties accurately. Every world map distorts at least one of them.

The projections shown here belong to three categories.

- **Conformal projections** show true shapes, but distort sizes. (You can remember this term's meaning by associating shape with the word *form* in conformal.)
- **Equal-area projections** show all areas in their true relative sizes, but distort shapes.
- **Compromise projections** allow some size distortions in order to portray shapes more accurately. In all types of world maps, distortion is generally least near the center and greatest at the edges.

Mercator

First published in 1569, the **Mercator** is a *conformal* projection. The poles are shown not as points, but as lines the same length as the Equator. The result is extreme size distortion in the higher latitudes. The Mercator was designed for navigation, and the true compass direction between any two points is shown by a straight line.

Gall–Peters

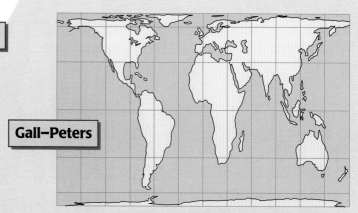

An *equal-area* projection first produced in the 1850s, the **Gall-Peters** greatly distorts shapes. Features near the Equator are stretched vertically, while features near the poles are flattened horizontally. The resulting shapes are quite different from those on a globe.

Armadillo

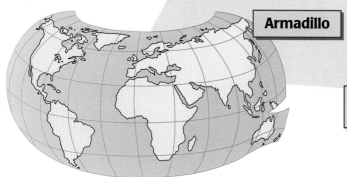

The **Armadillo** is a *compromise* projection intended to give young students the impression of a map being peeled from a globe. Because its unique appearance causes severe distortions, especially at the outer edges, it is seldom used outside the classroom.

Miller Cylindrical

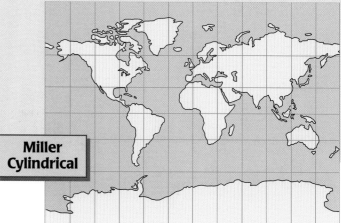

The **Miller** cylindrical is a *compromise* projection based on the Mercator. Its shapes are not as accurate as those of the Mercator, but it has much less size distortion. The Miller projection is often used when mapping world time zones.

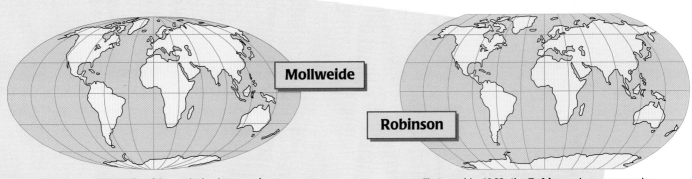

Mollweide

Robinson

The oval shape of the **Mollweide** reminds viewers of a globe. An *equal-area* projection, it is frequently used for world distribution maps. (A distribution map shows the location and extent of something—such as crops, livestock, or people—across the face of the earth.)

First used in 1963, the **Robinson** is a *compromise* projection. Because it presents a reasonable overall picture of the world, it is often used for educational materials. It looks similar to the Eckert IV (below), but has more distortion in the polar areas.

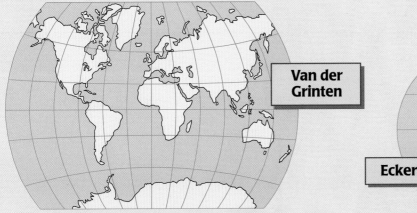

Van der Grinten

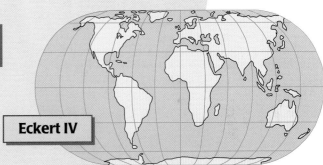

Eckert IV

The **Van der Grinten** is a *compromise* between the Mercator and the Mollweide. The full projection forms a circle, but the polar areas are normally not shown. Shapes and directions are reasonably accurate between 60°N and 60°S, where most of the world's people live.

An *equal-area* projection, the **Eckert IV** has relatively minor shape distortions near the Equator and poles. The result is a map well-suited either for general reference or for showing world distributions. It is often used to map world climates and other themes.

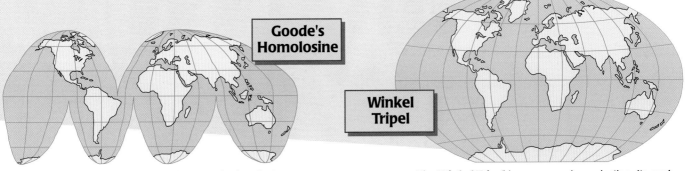

Goode's Homolosine

Winkel Tripel

The **Goode's Homolosine** is an *equal-area* projection that also shows shapes extremely well. Shapes can be shown more accurately than on most equal-area maps because the grid is interrupted or split in the ocean areas. The interruptions allow land areas to be shown with less stretch or distortion.

The **Winkel Tripel** is a *compromise* projection. Its oval shape and curving parallels result in a map with realistic shapes and minor size distortions at all latitudes. It has less size distortion than the Van der Grinten and less shape distortion than the Robinson.

GLOSSARY

Some of the definitions given below are followed by page numbers in parentheses. Photographs and special maps on those pages help illustrate the definitions.

Archipelago Group of islands.

Basin 1. Area drained by a river and its branches. 2. Area surrounded by higher land.

Bay Body of water partly surrounded by land and partly open to a larger body of water. The larger body of water can be an ocean, sea, or lake.

Bight Crescent-shaped indentation of a coastline, usually wider and more open than a bay.

Boreal forest Vast needleleaf forest located in cold regions of the Northern Hemisphere. (13H)

Broadleaf forest Forest whose trees have broad leaves. In places with cold winters, broad leaves change color and fall off each autumn. (13E, 19D, 61)

Canal Narrow waterway built for transportation or irrigation. (18C, 54)

Channel Passage of water connecting two larger bodies of water.

Climate Pattern of weather for a particular place or region in a typical year. (18–19)

Commercial farming Growing crops or raising livestock, largely for sale to others. (20A, 58, 73, 91)

Compass rose Set of pointers that show directions on a map or globe. (3)

Consumption Amount of a commodity that is used in a given amount of time.

Contiguous Connected or touching. The United States has 48 contiguous states plus Alaska and Hawaii.

Continent One of the seven largest land masses on earth.

Coral reef Extensive ridge or mound in the sea that consists of the outer skeletons of tiny sea animals. (103)

Cropland Region used mainly for growing crops. (12A, 24, 47, 67)

Cross section Drawing or special map that shows a section of the earth as seen from the side. Also known as a *profile drawing*. (54, 88–89)

Delta Vast accumulation of sediment at the mouth of a river. Often shaped like a triangle.

Deposit Concentration of rock, mineral, oil, or natural gas within the earth's crust.

Desert Dry region receiving little rain or snow and with little or no vegetation; usually hot. (12D, 18B, 59, 65)

Elevation Height above or below sea level of a place on land. (14–15, 28–29, 58)

Elevation map Map that uses color to show land elevations and, sometimes, water depths. (10–11, 42–43, 64)

Equator Imaginary line that divides the earth into northern and southern halves. The 0° line for measuring latitude.

Export Something that is sold to a buyer in another country.

Forestry Use of forests for lumber, paper, and other products.

Geyser Hot spring under such high pressure that it shoots water and steam into the air from time to time. (98)

Glacier Large body of ice formed from a long-lasting accumulation of snow on mountains and in polar regions. See **ice cap**. (13F, 88)

Grassland Region where grass grows, sometimes mixed with scattered shrubs or trees. Grasslands are often used for grazing. (12C, 30, 64)

Growing season Longest period when air temperatures stay above freezing. The time of year when crops can grow. (17)

Gulf Area of an ocean or sea partly surrounded by land.

Hemisphere Any half of the earth.

Highland Large area of mountains or elevated land. (19F, 91)

Ice cap Immense glacier covering much or all of a continent or very large island.

Ice shelf Large layer of ice attached to land and extending out onto the sea. (105)

Import Something that is bought from a seller in another country.

Irrigated land Land artificially supplied with water so crops can grow there.

Isthmus Narrow body of land connecting a continent with a peninsula or another continent.

Key Illustrated explanation of a map's symbols or colors. (3, 4)

Land cover Vegetation, deserts, and glaciers now covering the earth's land surface. (12–13)

Land cover map Map that uses color to show land cover, sea ice, and ocean floors. (6–7, 38–39)

Land use The main economic activity in an area. It is not the only activity, but it is the most significant or widespread. (20)

Landform Natural feature of the landscape, such as a mountain, plain, or island. (14–15)

Latitude Distance north or south of the Equator, as measured in degrees of a circle.

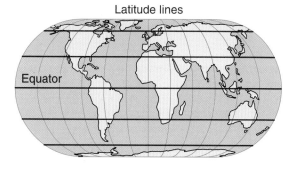
Latitude lines

Legend Illustrated explanation of a map's symbols, colors, and lettering styles. (3, 4)

Longitude Distance east or west of the Prime Meridian, as measured in degrees of a circle.

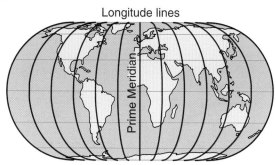
Longitude lines

Map projection Method of representing the earth's curved surface on a flat map. (106–107)

Monsoon Pattern of seasonal winds in Asia. The summer monsoon is wet, and the winter monsoon is dry. (90)

Natural gas Hydrocarbon gases formed underground when buried plants decompose. Natural gas can be burned to provide heat. (22, 47)

Needleleaf forest Forest of needleleaf trees, such as pines and other evergreens. (13H, 20D, 44)

Nomadic herding Raising herds of animals, moving them in a yearly cycle from one seasonal source of food and water to the next. (20D)

Ocean One of the five largest bodies of water on earth.

Peninsula Area of land that is almost surrounded by water.

Permafrost Ground that is frozen most or all of the year. (104)

Plain Broad area of land that is gently rolling or almost flat. (13H, 15, 81)

Plantation Extensive tract of land devoted mainly to one labor-intensive cash crop. (91)

Polar Related to or close to the North Pole or South Pole, or to the regions between the poles and the Arctic and Antarctic Circles. (19E, 104, 105)

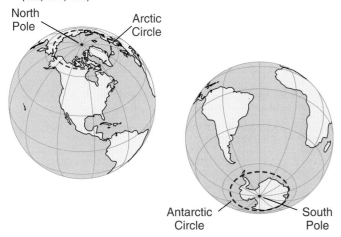

Political map Map that uses color to show countries, states, or other political divisions. (8–9, 34–35, 40–41)

Population People, especially those living in a particular place. *Population density* measures the population per square mile. (24–25)

Port Place where cargo or passengers are moved onto or off of ships. (94)

Prime Meridian Imaginary line that helps divide the earth into eastern and western halves. The 0° line for measuring longitude.

Production Amount of something manufactured, grown, or extracted from the land in a given amount of time.

Province Political division similar to a state. Canada has provinces rather than states. (34–35)

Rainfall Amount of water that falls at a place. Rainfall includes rain plus the water from melted snow, sleet, and hail. (16, 44)

Ranching and herding Raising herds of livestock on large, open ranches. The livestock graze or feed on the natural grasses that grow there. (20C, 30)

Range 1. A connected line of mountains. **2.** Vast grassland used for grazing. (15, 30)

Region Large area that is different from the areas around it. A region can be defined by a single feature or by several features, either natural or cultural. (45)

Resource Supply of something that can be used to meet needs and wants. (21, 22, 36)

Rural Belonging to the countryside, as opposed to cities. (24, 47, 91)

Scale Relationship between an actual distance on the earth and the same distance as shown on a map. (3)

Sea 1. One of the divisions of an ocean. **2.** Large inland body of salty water. **3.** All the oceans of the world.

Sea ice Ice floating on the sea. Some sea ice forms a nearly permanent cover, mainly near the North Pole, while other sea ice is seasonal. (104)

Sea level The average elevation of the world's oceans between high and low tide. (14)

Semi-desert Region covered by scattered vegetation but too dry for crops without irrigation. Also called *semi-arid*. (20C)

Shield Broad, level mass of rock close to the surface of the earth.

Steppes Dry grasslands and semi-deserts, especially those stretching from central Europe to southern Siberia in Asia. (15)

Strait Narrow passage of water connecting two larger bodies of water.

Subsistence farming Producing enough food for the farmers and their families, with little or none left over for sale to others. (20B, 67)

Suburban Relating to the ring of smaller towns that make up the outer part of an urban area. (25)

Summit The highest place on a mountain. (15, 44, 88)

Symbol Shape, picture, line, or color that is used on a map to stand for a region, place, feature, or characteristic. (3)

Tableland Elevated plain, usually with at least one steeply dropping or rising side; also called *plateau*. Some tablelands are heavily eroded. (14)

Territory 1. Part of a country that does not have the full rights of a state or province. **2.** Any large region, often with poorly defined boundaries.

Time zone Region that shares the same time of day, usually one hour earlier than the next zone to the west. (25)

Tropical rain forest Dense forest in or near the tropics that receives great amounts of rain and stays green throughout the year. (12B, 59, 98)

Tropics Warm middle zone of the earth lying between the Tropic of Cancer and the Tropic of Capricorn. (17, 18A)

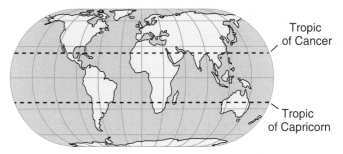

Tundra 1. Polar or mountainous area with no glaciers but too cold for trees to grow. **2.** Small plants that grow close to the ground in places that are cool or cold most of the year. (13G)

Upland Area of high ground, usually with a moderately hilly surface. (16)

Urban Consisting of cities or towns; the opposite of rural. Urban areas may be centers of manufacturing, trade, finance, or government. (25, 67, 92)

Weather Temperature, rainfall, and other conditions of the atmosphere over a short time. (16, 17)

Wetland Land where water is often at or near the surface. Bogs, marshes, and swamps are wetlands.

INDEX OF PLACES

T

U

Where Did Human Life Begin?

Many experts believe that our human species began in Africa 200,000 years ago. From there our early ancestors are thought to have slowly spread across the other continents.